Comparative Criminology

Recent Titles in
Research and Bibliographical Guides in Criminal Justice

Criminal Activity in the Deep South, 1700-1930: An Annotated Bibliography
A. J. Wright, compiler

Criminal Justice Ethics: Research and Bibliographical Guide
Frank Schmalleger, compiler, with the assistance of Robert McKenrick

COMPARATIVE CRIMINOLOGY

An Annotated Bibliography

COMPILED BY
Piers Beirne
AND
Joan Hill

Research and Bibliographical Guides in Criminal Justice, Number 3
Marilyn Lutzker, Series Adviser

Greenwood Press
New York • Westport, Connecticut • London

Library of Congress Cataloging-in-Publication Data

Beirne, Piers.
Comparative criminology : an annotated bibliography / compiled by Piers Beirne and Joan Hill.
p. cm.—(Research and bibliographical guides in criminal justice, ISSN 1042-4636 ; no. 3)
Includes indexes.
ISBN 0-313-26572-0 (lib. bdg. : alk. paper)
1. Criminology—Cross-cultural studies—Bibliography. I. Hill, Joan. II. Title. III. Series.
Z5703.B44 1991
[HV6025]
016.364—dc20 91-27306

British Library Cataloguing in Publication Data is available.

Library of Congress Catalog Card Number: 91-27306
ISBN: 0-313-26572-0
ISSN: 1042-4636

First published in 1991

Greenwood Press, 88 Post Road West, Westport, CT 06881
An imprint of Greenwood Publishing Group, Inc.

Printed in the United States of America

The paper used in this book complies with the Permanent Paper Standard issued by the National Information Standards Organization (Z39.48-1984).

10 9 8 7 6 5 4 3 2 1

Contents

APPENDICES

Preface

PURPOSE

The purpose of this bibliography is to provide researchers and students with a useful list of annotated references in comparative criminology. Because criminologists have tended to ignore the comparative dimensions of their discipline, only recently has the compilation of such a bibliography become a worthwhile enterprise. No more than two or three decades ago, during the 1950s and 1960s, a concerted program of comparative research on crime, law, and social control was entirely absent from criminology. According to a well-known survey of comparative sociology by Robert Marsh (see #054; and see #008), for example, from 1950 to 1963 only a tiny fraction of journal articles in sociology, social anthropology, and social psychology dealt with the broad area of conformity and deviance. Of this fraction, only a small number systematically compared the phenomena of crime and social control in two or more cultures.

The recent surge of interest in comparative criminology, which this bibliography documents, can be attributed to a variety of factors. The two most significant ones should be mentioned here. First, among criminologists of assorted intellectual and political leanings, there has been a growing realization that much existing criminological theory is very limited in both its scope and its explanatory power. To date, the great bulk of the labors of criminologists has emanated from only a few western countries. Drawing on lessons established in the philosophy and history of science, criminologists now understand that the explanatory power of theories can be enhanced considerably if they are systematically tested under as diverse temporal and cultural conditions as possible. Comparative criminology occupies this pivotal experimental role. Second, and strongly tied to the first factor, during the last decade criminology has seen something of a weakening in the global dominance traditionally exercised by researchers and practitioners in the United States. Criminologists in many parts of the world have started visibly to challenge or to oppose the notion that criminological theories produced in the United States are necessarily applicable elsewhere. This tendency has been especially true in Canada, Australia, New Zealand, parts of

Western Europe, Africa, and Latin America. It has led to renewed interest in the cultural specificity of one's own theories, in the criminology of other countries, and in trying to discover if, how, and what the one can learn from the other.

SCOPE

No bibliography of comparative criminology can be entirely free of the cultural idiosyncrasies of those who compile it. We therefore feel it is necessary to provide some perspective on the scope of its contents. First and foremost, by the term "comparative criminology" we refer to the systematic study of crime, law, and social control in two or more cultures. Thus, we have tended to exclude from the bibliography those "single-culture" studies which focus on issues in a single culture and which, thereby, have no obvious comparative intent.

This bibliography covers literature that has been significant in the field of comparative criminology and that has been of continuing interest since the 1960s. Readers will notice, however, that the great majority of the entries were published after the early 1970s. It contains 500 entries, representing an extensive search of the fields of criminology, criminal justice, the anthropology of law, the sociology of law, and the sociology of social control. The entries cover a variety of sources and include books, chapters in books, professional journal articles, conference and symposium proceedings, and a few unpublished papers.

It must be emphasized that most of the entries in this bibliography were originally published in the English language. Although we originally intended to include works published in other languages, it soon became clear that the realization of such a desirable objective was quite impractical, even with reasonable language skills. We have opted for a bibliography whose focus is clearly defined in advance, a bibliography of comparative criminology compiled primarily for the benefit of an English-language audience.

The bibliography reveals that there are still enormous gaps in the literature on comparative criminology, which can be seen from even a cursory reading of the entries in several of the chapters. Very little comparative research has been conducted on economic and political crime, for example, or on transnational corporate crime. Virtually nothing at all has been published on the circumstances under which states commit crimes against their own populations or against the populations of other countries.

ORGANIZATION

The bibliography is organized into three Parts. Each Part reflects a major dimension of comparative criminology. Part I (*Meaning and Measurement in Comparative Criminology*) contains a variety of entries that deal with key issues in the comparative study of crime. The entries in Part II (*Cross-National Crime Rates*) address a number of relatively discrete areas in comparative criminology. Part III (*Social Control and Criminal Justice*) attends to the coercive features of social control, of law, and of criminal justice.

Chapter 1 ("General Issues in Comparative Criminology") introduces a variety of fundamental questions that confront comparative study. Some of these entries address the comparative enterprise in general. How can other cultures be understood? How can they be compared? What can be gained from so doing? Other entries refer to basic issues in comparative criminology itself. Does what is defined as criminal tend to be defined in the same way in different cultures? Can we compare crime rates in different cultures if the legal definitions of crime vary from one culture to another? What is the goal of comparative criminology?

Chapter 2 ("Cross-National Crime Data") provides information about the empirical data that are available for the study of cross-national crime rates. These include both the official data of national and international bodies and the unofficial data gathered in victimization surveys or in historical studies. Many of the entries discuss the weaknesses and the strengths of cross-national crime data.

Chapter 3 ("Perceptions of Crime") examines the question of whether different cultures regard offenses with the same degree of seriousness. Is the theft of a bicycle in Ireland, for example, viewed with the same degree of censure as it is in Kuwait or in the U.S.? Indeed, how does one measure 'seriousness' in cross-cultural analysis?

Chapter 4 ("Violent Crime") contains by far the largest number of entries of any substantive area in comparative criminology. The diverse backgrounds of the authors whose work is annotated here comprise sociology, criminal justice, law, history, political science, social work, economics, philosophy, psychology, and psychiatry. The substantive topics include homicide, historical studies of collective violence, violence against women and children, drinking and driving (not always, but often, a crime with violent consequences), and the subculture of violence thesis.

Chapter 5 ("Crimes Against Property") outlines the extant cross-cultural research on common crimes against property, of which there is precious little. Topics include robbery and burglary, with some interesting lessons to be drawn from the cases of Switzerland and Sweden. Those wishing to pursue this area further should dig deeply into the victimization survey entries listed in Chapter 2.

Chapter 6 ("Economic and Political Crime") summarizes the few comparative studies of what are often termed 'the crimes of the powerful'. Under the rubric 'economic crime', readers will recognize the familiar categories of white-collar crime and organized crime. The term 'political crime' should embrace not only the obvious entries on 'terrorism' but also crimes by states and by state officials; however, the dearth of comparative entries on the latter shows that comparative criminology has made no inroads there to date.

Chapter 7 ("Transnational Corporate Crime") addresses an area of great importance to comparative criminology, but one that has not yet been examined with sufficient attention. Doubtless, this category will be expanded in the future by those who are concerned with the exploitation of the Third World in terms of the global penetration of capital.

Chapter 8 ("Correlates of Crime: Age, Class, Gender and Race") contains numerous entries that address the influence of age, class, gender, and race on crime. Of these the majority concern age (youth rather than the elderly), although comparative studies of gender and crime are also quite well represented.

Chapter 9 ("Underdevelopment and Modernization") contains entries from two competing, and quite hostile, perspectives on the relationship between social and economic change and crime. "Underdevelopment theory" tends to see many crime patterns in the Third World as a result of the penetration of external capital. "Modernization theory" tends to see events in the Third World as a replay of the history of First World societies. It would be interesting to speculate about how modernization theory could account for the implications of transnational corporate crime, but that is not possible here.

Chapter 10 ("Social Control and Dispute Resolution") refers to an area of enormous significance that until quite recently has been ignored in comparative criminology. It contains entries regarding the diverse ways in which social control and law structure the nature of disputes -- some of which are defined as crimes -- and their adjudication.

Chapter 11 ("Criminal Justice and Penal Policies") contains two sorts of entries. The first addresses the institutions of criminal justice in comparative perspective, especially the police and incarceration. The second compares the effects of various penal policies on crime rates. Is there comparative evidence that violence, for example, can be reduced by economic policies rather than by repressive penal policies? Do repressive penal policies merely contribute to the perpetuation of the very problem that they are ostensibly designed to eliminate?

CITATION FORMAT AND CONTENT OF ENTRIES

The entries in this bibliography follow a standard format. Each entry begins with the name of the author(s), and it then provides date of publication, full title of the work, and place and date of publication, along with information about the number of pages in the work, notes, and bibliography. The entry contains a summary of the major points of the work, its sources and methodology, and its findings. Some entries refer the reader to other entries in the bibliography, for example '[and see #666]'.

In nearly all cases we have resisted the great urge to evaluate the intellectual merits of the entries in the bibliography. The content of the entries is intended to be purely descriptive.

ACKNOWLEDGEMENTS

The impetus for compiling this bibliography came from our participation in an ongoing seminar in comparative criminology at the University of Southern Maine. The student members of that seminar were the first to impress on us the need for an annotated bibliography such as this, and we remain indebted to them for their persistence. Cassandra Fitzherbert and Jim Brady were models of patience and good cheer when confronted with our numerous and sometimes incoherent requests for bibliographic advice. Thanks also to Loraine A. Lowell and John Plante. Shelly Kellis valiantly performed some of the time-consuming work of formatting and indexing, and her efforts are much appreciated. Casey Groves, Marilyn Lutzker, Mildred Vasan, Graeme Newman, Michael Lynch, Beth Kempler Pfannl, Peter Lehman and Jill Kendall offered their expertise at the right moments. The tedium of compiling the bibliography was somewhat relieved by a small grant provided us by the College of Arts and Sciences at the University of Southern Maine.

PART I

MEANING AND MEASUREMENT IN COMPARATIVE CRIMINOLOGY

1

General Issues in Comparative Criminology

001. Abel, Richard L. (1973). "A Comparative Theory of Dispute Institutions in Society," *Law & Society Review*, 8(2):217-347. Notes, bibliography.

An influential article inspired by the author's analysis of the legal system in Kenya, a pluralistic society experiencing rapid social change under the impact of colonialism. Investigates the complex cross-cultural problems involved in defining the concepts of law, legal and political disputes, dispute processes, and interveners. Offers a formal theory of the dispute process and its institutions. Contains a mass of comparative material drawn from anthropology, history, and sociology.

002. Abel, Richard L. (1978). "Comparative Law and Social Theory," *American Journal of Comparative Law*, 26:219-226. Notes.

Proceeds from a discussion of reforms, stability, and change in Islamic family law to analyze the purpose of comparative law and its relationship to social theory. Addresses the ambiguous and complex nature of law and describes several theoretical frameworks in order to question the validity of an influential thesis about family law.

003. Abi-Saab, Georges (1989). "The Concept of International Crimes and its Place in Contemporary International Law." Pp.141-150 in Joseph H.H. Weiler, Antonio Cassese, and Marina Spinedi (eds.), *International Crimes of State: A Critical Analysis of the ILC's Draft Article on State Responsibility.* Berlin: Walter de Gruyter.

Attempts to examine objectively the legal status, rationale, and sociological underpinnings in contemporary international law. Outlines historical, sociological, and technical levels of analysis. Discusses the definitional criteria and legal effects of the concept of international crimes and possible objections to it.

004. Almond, Gabriel A., and G. Bingham Powell, Jr. (1966). *Comparative Politics: A Developmental Approach.* Boston, Massachusetts: Little, Brown. Notes, xv + 348pp.

Compares functions of political systems from three perspectives: (1) conversion functions, (2) the operation of the political system, and (3) the maintenance and adaptation of political systems. Discusses relationships among structure, culture and government operations, and political development. Categorizes primitive, traditional, democratic, and authoritarian political systems.

005. Alper, Benedict S., and Jerry F. Boren (1972). *Crime: International Agenda.* Lexington, Massachusetts: Lexington Books and D.C. Heath. Bibliography, xxii + 220pp.

Outlines and reviews international academic gatherings (1846-1970) where criminological issues were discussed. Classifies discussions, evolving perspectives, international organizations, and analyses.

006. Armer, Michael, and Allen D. Grimshaw (eds.) (1973). *Comparative Social Research: Methodological Problems and Strategies.* New York: John Wiley. Notes, bibliographies, xxi + 473pp.

Contains 15 chapters on various aspects of comparative research, comparative methods, the nature of comparative analysis and interpretation, and cross-cultural research conditions. Several chapters illustrate cross-cultural methodological problems and possibilities. Chapter 3 discusses field difficulties. Chapter 4 addresses interview difficulties in India.

007. Beirne, Piers (1983). "Cultural Relativism and Comparative Criminology," *Contemporary Crises*, 7(4): 371-391. Bibliography.

Outlines various methodological and epistemological difficulties encountered in comparing the extent and meaning of crime in countries that are respectively similar, that are similar in some respects, and that are largely dissimilar.

008. Beirne, Piers (1983). "Generalization and Its Discontents: The Comparative Study of Crime." Pp.19-38 in Israel L. Barak-Glantz and Elmer H. Johnson (eds.), *Comparative Criminology.* Beverly Hills, California: Sage. Notes, bibliography.

Discusses fundamental difficulties of methods, concepts, and theories in comparative criminology. Reviews origins of comparative criminology and criticizes the three methodologies most often used in U.S. comparative analysis. Briefly proposes a comparative framework.

009. Beirne, Piers and James W. Messerschmidt (1991). *Criminology.* New York: Harcourt Brace Jovanovich. Bibliography, xxi + 682pp.

Chapter 16 ("Comparative Criminology") provides an overall view regarding the promise of comparative criminology and of the methodological and theoretical difficulties involved in achieving it. Substantive topics include crime and underdevelopment, the alleged commonalities among countries with low crime rates, the modernization thesis, generalizations about the respective crime rates of capitalist and socialist societies, and U.S. penal policies in comparative perspective.

010. Bendix, Reinhard (1963). "Concepts and Generalizations in Comparative Sociological Studies," *American Sociological Review*, 28(4): 532-539. Notes.

Discusses several problems related to the lack of continuity in most sociological concepts and theories. Reviews the difficulties and limitations concerning the methodological validity and theoretical generalization of historical and comparative concepts. Exemplifies comparative sociological characteristics and their uses.

011. Bendix, Richard (1968). "Concepts in Comparative Historical Analysis." Pp.67-81 in Stein Rokkan (ed.), *Comparative Research Across Cultures and Nations*. Paris: Mouton. Notes.

Introduces a conceptual method of analysis for examining comparative historical change. Points to evolutionism, systems theory, and social engineering as three methods used to study historical change and discusses the limitations of each model when attempting to identify universal concepts. Advocates the use of concepts relevant to societies under comparison.

012. Bennett, Richard R. (1980). "Constructing Cross-Cultural Theories in Criminology: Application of the Generative Approach," *Criminology*, 18(2): 252-268. Notes, bibliography.

Examines the comparative method as an antidote to the cultural myopia of generalizations about crime generated in the context of a single culture. Distinguishes between 'evaluative' and 'generative' approaches to theory construction, using police occupational solidarity as a cross-cultural example of the latter apoproach. Addresses limitations and advantages of the comparative method.

013. Blazicek, Donald L. (1980). "Promises or Pitfalls: Prospectus on Comparative Victimology," *International Journal of Comparative and Applied Criminal Justice*, 4(1):85-94. Bibliography.

Advocates comparative victimological research and theory. Discusses the need for comparative victimological research and the importance of examining the interaction among victim, perpetrator, and the criminal justice system. Reviews relevant victimological literature and data. Addresses methodological difficulties.

014. Bohannan, Paul (1965). "The Differing Realms of the Law," *American Anthropologist*, 65(6): 33-42. Bibliography.

Examines legal definitions, the relationships among customs, norms and legal systems ('double institutionalization'), and the use of the political state as an enforcement mechanism. Outlines differing realms of law, including municipal systems, colonial law in unicentric power systems, law in stateless societies, and international law in bicentric or multicentric power systems.

015. Buchholz, E., R. Hartmann, J. Lekschas, and G. Stiller (1974). *Socialist Criminology: Theory and Methodology.* Westmead, Hampshire: Saxon House. Appendix, v + 413pp.

Argues for the importance of socialist criminology. Arguments are woven around the advantages of dialectical analysis and criticisms of bourgeois criminology. Chapters address crime in the Federal Republic of Germany, the criminal personality, and the methodology of criminological research.

016. Chambliss, William J. and Robert B. Seidman (1970). *Sociology of the Law: A Research Bibliography.* Berkeley, California: Glendessary Press. 113pp.

Bibliography of the sociology of law. Contains chapters on general sociology of law; legal history; jurisprudence; legal profession; private law; commerce, industry, and business planning; social welfare and labor law; public law and constitutional law; administrative law; criminal law; administration of justice; impact of legal sanctions; and comparative legal systems and international law.

017. Chang, Dae H. (ed.) (1976). *Criminology: A Cross-Cultural Perspective.* 2 vols. Durham, North Carolina: Carolina Academic Press. Notes, bibliographies, indices, xiv + 1039pp.

Volume 1 has a brief history of comparative criminology. The remainder of volume 1 and all of volume 2 contain many single-culture descriptions of crime and delinquency, including organizational, geographic and historical features; typologies; and police and court functions. Countries include Argentina, Czechoslovakia, Canada, Ethiopia, Federal Republic of Germany, Italy, Japan, Malaysia, the Philippines, the U.S., and Venezuela.

018. Christie, Nils (1970). "Comparative Criminology," *Canadian Journal of Corrections*, 12: 40-46.

Discusses the many theoretical problems of comparative criminology. Proposes an aggregate study of societies. Details various methodological and cultural difficulties, such as the unreliability of official police statistics and cross-cultural variation in meaning. Outlines suggestions for future comparative inquiry, including social systems analysis, systematic comparative criminological research, and behavioral and trend analysis.

019. Clifford, W. (1965). "Problems in Criminological Research in Africa South of the Sahara," *International Review of Criminal Policy*, 23: 11-17. Notes.

Discusses the numerous research difficulties in the study of crime which hinder cross-national analysis. Focus is the lack of systematic official crime records and of consensus about concepts of crime in social science, particularly in psychiatry, sociology, and criminology in Africa. Proposes a research agenda.

020. Clifford, W. (1975). "New Dimensions in Criminality -- National and Transnational," *Australian and New Zealand Journal of Criminology*, 8(2): 67-85. Notes.

Questions whether national and transnational crime variations should be conceptualized as new facts or as transformations of long-existing crime patterns. Outlines criteria for new dimensions of criminality. Discusses relationships among modern society, social attitudes, laws, institutions, social change, and crime. Reports global increases in crime in Europe, the U.S., Bangladesh, Turkey, Nepal, Hong Kong, India, Pakistan, Malta, Zambia, Costa Rica, the Bahamas, Sri Lanka, the Caribbean, Argentina and Italy.

021. Clifford, W. (1977). "Culture and Crime," *Annales Internationales de Criminologie*, 16(1-2): 87108. Bibliography.

Discusses the relationship between culture and crime and the ethnocentric role of criminology in exporting western crime philosophies to non-western cultures. Focus is the extant neglect of comparativism in criminology and the need for cross-cultural and subcultural analysis and world crime perspective. Discusses problems of cross-cultural research, including indicators of culture and crime.

022. Clifford, William (1983). "Criminology in Developing Nations -- African and Asian Examples." Pp. 83-98 in Elmer H. Johnson (ed.), *International Handbook of Contemporary Developments in Criminology: General Issues and the Americas*. Westport, Connecticut: Greenwood Press. Notes, bibliography.

Exemplifies African and Asian criminology to demonstrate the cultural differences in crime patterns, and their interpretation, in developed and in developing nations. Questions the relationships among politics, economics, and crime in developed and developing nations. Stresses cultural variations in the meaning of crime.

023. Diamond, Stanley (1971). "The Rule of Law Versus the Order of Custom," *Social Research*, 38(1): 42-72.

An important and widely-read examination of Paul Bohannan's [see # 014] thesis of the relationship between law and custom. Emphasizes differences between law and custom. Discusses the historical, legal, and social aspects of law and society, the significance of customary rule and its transmission to modern societies.

024. Dixon, Keith (1977). "Is Cultural Relativism Self-Refuting?" *British Journal of Sociology*, 28(1): 75-88. Notes.

Outlines various methodological and epistemological contours of cultural relativism. Reviews several relativist approaches in anthropology, social philosophy, and sociology. Criticizes relativist claims and also the notion that cultural relativism might be self-refuting.

025. Edgerton, Robert B. (1976). *Deviance: A Cross-Cultural Perspective*. Menlo Park, California: Cummings Publishing. Bibliography, 133pp.

Offers a history of explanations of deviance. Uses a mass of anthropological material from folk and urban societies to provide comparative generalizations about theft, suicide, violence, sexuality, generational conflict, psychoactive drugs, mental retardation, and mental illness. Examines the influence on rates of deviance of biology, temperament, human nature, and society.

026. Fenwick, Charles R. (1984). *Curriculum and Course Development Project: International Criminal Justice Systems.* Omaha, Nebraska: Academy of Criminal Justice Sciences. Bibliographies, 115pp.

Outlines cross-cultural criminal justice curricula and course focus and development offered by various colleges and univer-sities. Provides course syllabi and comprehensive references which include reading and visual sources.

027. Ferracuti, Franco and Marvin E. Wolfgang (eds.) (1983). *Criminological Diagnosis: An International Perspective.* 2 vols. Toronto: Lexington Books and D.C. Heath. Notes, bibliography, xi + 619pp.

Contains 17 essays on contemporary diagnostic practices and theoretical views regarding crime in Argentina, Italy, Japan, Egypt, Spain, Denmark, Norway, Israel, Yugoslavia, the U.S.S.R., England, and the U.S.

028. Flynn, Edith E. (1977). "Issues and Priorities in International Cooperation in the Field of Criminology," *Annales Internationales de Criminologie*,16(1-2): 13-40.

Summarizes conference proceedings of the International Seminar on Issues and Priorities held in Italy in May, 1976. The seminar's stated purpose was to discuss international academic cooperation in criminology, to explore areas of comparative study, and to determine research priorities. Topical outlines include the assessment of crime as a problem, its prevention and control, the operation of criminal justice systems, professional ethics and human rights, and comparative research.

029. Friday, Paul (1983). "International Organizations: An Introduction." Pp. 31-36 in vol.2 of Elmer H. Johnson (ed.), *International Handbook of Contemporary Developments in Criminology: General Issues and the Americas.* 2 vols. Westport, Connecticut: Greenwood Press.

Describes the evolution and advancement of international criminological organizations and the theoretical changes in criminology following World War II. Traces the development of international organizations and the expansion of criminological perspectives worldwide.

030. Friday, Paul C. (1973). "Problems in Comparative Criminology: Comments on the Feasibility and Implications of Research," *International Journal of Criminology and Penology*, 1(2): 151-160. Notes, bibliography.

Addresses the need for integration and synthesis in comparative criminology. Identifies numerous methodological problems in comparative criminology. Reviews two classifications of methodological approaches (domestic and comparative) and their advantages and disadvantages. Discusses the social, political, and professional problems facing comparativists.

031. Glueck, Sheldon (1964). "Wanted: A Comparative Criminology." Pp.304-322 in Sheldon and Eleanor Glueck (eds.), *Ventures in Criminology: Selected Recent Papers*. Cambridge, Massachusetts: Harvard University Press. Notes.

Attempts to demonstrate the need for a systematic comparative criminology. Exemplifies some central issues in comparative criminology. Discusses the uses of scientific comparative analysis and prediction, particularly in criminal justice administration, crime prevention, and rehabilitation programs. Reviews various areas worthy of comparative investigation, including the etiology of crime and interdisciplinary concepts.

032. Grimshaw, Allen D. (1973). "Comparative Sociology: In What Ways Different From Other Sociologies?" Pp.3-48 in Michael Armer and Allen D. Grimshaw (eds.), *Comparative Social Research: Methodological Problems and Strategies*. New York: John Wiley. Notes, bibliography.

Introductory essay focusing on the systematic differences between comparative sociology and other areas of sociology. Describes comparative sociology as an attempt to identify universals and typologies. Discusses problems related to language and meaning.

033. Groves, W. Byron, and Graeme Newman (1989). "Against General Theory in Comparative Research," *International Journal of Comparative and Applied Criminal Justice*, 13(1): 23-29. Bibliography.

Challenges the search for a universal theory of crime. Criticizes Shelley's [see # 347] views on generalization. Offers three propositions for proper theory construction: (1) the absence of a priori conditions for theory, (2) a close relationship between concepts and content, and (3) theoretical recognition of historical specificity.

034. Gutteridge, H.C. (1971). *Comparative Law: An Introduction to the Comparative Method of Legal Study and Research*. London: Wildy. Appendix, xv + 214pp.

Traces the origin, development, and value of comparative law. Addresses public and private international law and comparative legal and research methodology. Focus is comparative legal approach to case law, the process of legal comparison, and statute interpretation. Outlines differences between common and civil law.

035. Hippchen, Leonard J. (1981). "Importance of Teaching the International Aspects of Criminal Justice," *International Journal of Comparative and Applied Criminal Justice*, 5(2): 221-227. Bibliography.

Discusses the need for teaching international perspectives of criminal justice, especially for those in criminology and related disciplines. Outlines rationale for the development of comparative criminal justice analysis, including rising crime rates in many parts of the world, the investigation of cross-cultural criminal justice systems, and crime prevention methods. Provides recommendations for course study.

036. Hollander, Paul (1973). *Soviet and American Society: A Comparison*. New York: Oxford University Press. Notes, bibliography, xx + 476pp.

Macro-sociological comparative analysis of Soviet and U.S. cultures. Focus is Soviet and U.S. political institutions and practices, cultural values, and social problems. Chapter 8 compares crime and delinquency in both countries. Comparative evaluations include crime types, juvenile delinquency and punishment, theories of crime, and cultural contradictions. Reviews theoretical and methodological problems.

037. Hollander, Paul (1975). "Comparing Socialist Systems: Ends and Results." Pp.421-436 in Carmelo Mesa-Lago and Carl Beck (eds.), *Comparative Socialist Systems: Essays on Politics and Economics*. Pittsburgh, Pennsylvania: University of Pittsburgh Center for International Studies. Notes.

Discusses the nature of comparative analysis, with emphasis on comparing socialist systems. Addresses Eastern European developments and the need for interdisciplinary comparative focus, especially in socialist societies with little available data. Outlines prolific comparative research areas: socialist social systems, social problems, and values and beliefs. Briefly reviews other essays in the book.

038. Holt, Robert T., and John E. Turner (1970). "The Methodology of Comparative Research." Pp.1-20 in Robert T. Holt and John E. Turner (eds.), *The Methodology of Comparative Research*. New York: The Free Press. Notes, bibliography.

An introductory chapter that clarifies the methodological and theoretical goals of comparative political research. Focus is the appropriate application of the comparative research method and the need for cross-cultural analysis. Outlines several methodological approaches. Discusses various methodological and conceptual difficulties in examining dissimilar cultures.

039. Holt, Robert T., and John M. Richardson, Jr.(1970). "Competing Paradigms in Comparative Politics." Pp.21-71 in Robert T. Holt and John E. Turner (eds.), *The Methodology of Comparative Research*. New York: The Free Press. Notes.

Focus is the theoretical aspects of comparative politics. Outlines the fundamental nature and operation of science and its intrinsic relationship to conceptual analysis and theory construction. Examines five basic approaches to political theory, including structural-functionalism, systems analysis, psychological approaches, rationalist models, and atheoretical approaches.

040. Holyst, Brunon (1979). *Comparative Criminology*. Lexington, Massachusetts: Lexington Books and D. C. Heath. Bibliography, xiii + 409pp.

A comprehensive study integrating various aspects of comparative criminology. Emphasizes cross-cultural theoretical and methodological issues. Chapter 10 discusses research in the developing countries of Africa, the Middle East and southeast Asia. Chapter 11 focuses on criminology in Latin America. Outlines international crime institutions and organizations.

041. Holyst, Brunon (1985). "The Role of Criminological Research in Shaping Social Policy." Pp.379-387 in Pedro R. David (ed.), *Crime and Criminal Policy*. Pub. 25. Milan: United Nations Social Defence Research Institute.

Identifies significant relationships among criminology, the design of criminal justice systems, and socioeconomic and political policy. Argues for a new criminology that advocates interdisciplinary training and broad analytical focus. Outlines two social policy functions and two remedial methods which might enhance social development.

042. Hymes, Dell (1970). "Linguistic Aspects of Comparative Political Research." Pp. 295-341 in Robert T. Holt and John E. Turner (eds.), *The Methodology of Comparative Research.* New York: The Free Press. Notes.

Addresses the question of whether, and if so how, linguistic problems affect the comparative study of politics. Discusses the various methodological difficulties and possibilities of comparative political science analysis.

043. Inciardi, James A., Alan A. Block, and Lyle A. Hallowell (1977). *Historical Approaches to Crime: Research Strategies and Issues.* Beverly Hills, California: Sage. Bibliography, appendices, 215pp.

Discusses the theory and methodology of historical approaches to the study of crime. Part 1 outlines various methodologies of historical analysis. Part 2 discusses the relationships among history, folklore and legend, and evaluation difficulties therein. Explores the 'Wild West' era of U.S. history and women's roles in organized crime during the Progressive Era. Part III discusses historical concepts of time. Appendices serve as reference literature.

044. Janeksela, Galan (1977). "Typologies in Comparative Criminal Justice Research," *International Journal of Comparative and Applied Criminal Justice*, 1(2): 103-110. Notes, bibliography.

Discusses the universal need of a formal typology to study crime, law, and criminal justice from a comparative perspective. Describes the relationship of theory to typologies. Emphasizes universality of theories and compares sub-system types in Eastern and Western countries. Outlines Romano-Germanic, common law, socialist law, and religious and traditional law typologies.

045. Jarvie, I.C. (1983). "Rationality and Relativism," *British Journal of Sociology*, 34(1): 44-60. Notes and references.

Critically discusses the philosophical conflict between relativist and rationalist doctrines. Offers a theoretical compromise through a strategy of weak absolutism, allowing cultural and cross-cultural comparabilty and toleration. Reviews rationalist and relativist tenets and relevant philosophical concepts.

046. Johnson, Elmer H. (1983). "Criminology: Its Variety and Patterns Throughout the World." Pp.5-30 in vol. 2 of Elmer H. Johnson (ed.), *International Handbook of Contemporary Developments in Criminology: General Issues and the Americas.* 2 vols. Westport, Connecticut: Greenwood Press. Bibliography.

Addresses the importance of cross-cultural analysis for criminology. Discusses the advantages of comparative investigation of social, political, and legal systems to the study of criminology; the methodological problems of comparative analysis; and the growing interest in contemporary comparative research.

047. Johnson, Elmer H. (ed.) (1983). *International Handbook of Contemporary Developments in Criminology, vol. 1 : General Issues and the Americas.* Westport, Connecticut: Greenwood Press. xvi + 319pp.

The seven essays in Part 1 focus on an eclectic set of themes, including official and unofficial international organizations of criminology, criminology in Asia and Africa, women and criminology, and radical criminology. The seven essays in Part 2 are single-culture studies of the Americas, including Argentina, Brazil, Canada, Chile, Costa Rica, Mexico, and the U.S. Focus is the state of criminology and research in each culture.

048. Johnson, Elmer H. (ed.) (1983). *International Handbook of Contemporary Developments in Criminology, vol. 2 : Europe, Africa, the Middle East and Asia.* Westport, Connecticut: Greenwood Press. Annotations, xx + 696pp.

Contains 31 single-culture essays on criminology in various European, African, Middle Eastern, and Asian countries. Each essay describes the dominant form of criminology, education, and the organizational, social, cultural, economic, and political climate.

049. Kohn, Melvin L. (ed.) (1989). *Cross-National Research in Sociology.* Newbury Park, California: Sage. Notes, bibliographies, 424pp.

The 17 essays in this volume address a wide variety of issues in comparative sociology, many of which have theoretical relevance for comparative criminology. Themes include conceptual and methodological issues; studies on Max Weber; and the nation as context for primary, secondary, multinational, and transnational analyses.

050. Lijphart, Arend (1971). "Comparative Politics and the Comparative Method," *American Political Science Review,* 65(3): 682-693. Notes.

Outlines and compares the experimental, statistical, and comparative method of political analysis. Critically discusses the weaknesses, strengths, limitations and possibilities of comparative investigation and its relationship to theory construction.

051. López-Rey, Manuel (1970). *Crime: An Analytical Appraisal.* New York: Praeger. Notes, xiv + 277pp.

Addresses the need to study crime as a sociopolitical phenomenon and as a social problem. Focuses on crime and the development of criminal policy and reviews relevant theories of crime and delinquency. Chapter 4 addresses international relationships among population growth, World War II, and rising crime rates. Provides some comparative demographic data about male/female crime ratios for England and Wales, the Federal Republic of Germany, Spain, Norway, Yugoslavia, the United States, Canada, Argentina, the U.S.S.R., and various Arab nations.

052. Lorwin, Val R. (1968). "Historians and Other Social Scientists: The Comparative Analysis of Nation-Building in Western Societies." Pp.102-117 in Stein Rokkan (ed.), *Comparative Research Across Cultures and Nations*. Paris: Mouton. Notes.

Identifies the types of historical analysis which further comparative nation-building inquiry (one-nation studies) and cross-cultural analysis. Discusses interdisciplinary collaboration and contemporary interdisciplinary studies of small-scale European societies such as Ireland, Austria, Switzerland, The Netherlands, and the Scandinavian countries.

053. Mannheim, Herman (1965). *Comparative Criminology*. 2 vols. London: Routledge & Kegan Paul. Notes, appendix, 793pp.

These two volumes are often represented as a pioneering effort in comparative criminology, but there is very little genuinely comparative in them. Volume 1 discusses criminological, legal, and customary concepts of crime, various research methods, and crime-related features. Volume 2 critically analyzes the relationship of social class to crime in Britain and discusses class and non-class criminological theories and various social factors such as primary group association, age, and gender.

054. Marsh, Robert M. (1967). *Comparative Sociology: A Codification of Cross-Societal Analysis*. New York: Harcourt, Brace & World. Appendix, annotated bibliography, xvi + 527pp.

Identifies the paucity of comparative studies of crime and justice prior to the mid-1960s. Discusses the importance of systematic cross-cultural sociological and anthropological analysis and its relationship to the construction of theoretical generalizations. Various methodological problems are addressed and cross-cultural studies examined.

055. Marshall, Ineke Haen, and Chris E. Marshall (1983). "Toward a Refinement of Purpose in Comparative Criminological Research: Research Site Selection in Focus," *International Journal of Comparative and Applied Criminal Justice*, 7(1): 89-97. Bibliography.

Challenges the careless merging of comparative research objectives. Outlines two aims of comparative research: theory testing the universality of a proposition, and theory construction of a specified proposition. Discusses the difficulties of comparing dissimilar cultures. Advocates research in comparable Western societies for theory construction, and in dissimilar societies for theory testing.

056. Miller, Delbert C. (1973). "Design Strategies for Comparative International Studies of Community Power." Pp.193-216 in Michael Armer and Allen D. Grimshaw (eds.), *Comparative Social Research: Methodological Problems and Strategies*. New York: John Wiley. Notes, bibliography.

Examines basic comparative problems of studying international social and political systems. Outlines the Community Power System Model and uses it to examine the relationship of institutionalized community power structures to institutionalized nation power structures between 1953-1966 in Seattle (Washington), Bristol (England), Cordoba (Argentina), and Lima

(Peru). Reviews various methodological approaches, relevant literature, and findings.

057. Miracle, Andrew W. Jr. (1981). "Cross-Cultural Research and the Role of Anthropology in Criminal Justice," *Journal of Criminal Justice*, 9: 383-388. Bibliography.

Assesses the availability and geographical distribution of cross-cultural research on non-western crime. Uses International Journal of Criminology and Penology, International Journal of Comparative and Applied Criminal Justice, British Journal of Criminology, and Social Science Citation Index, 1972-1979. Objects to the lack of comparative study of non-western cultures and advocates the role of anthropology in criminal justice research and theory.

058. Newman, Graeme R. (ed.) (1980). *Crime and Deviance: A Comparative Perspective*. Beverly Hills, California: Sage. Notes, bibliographies, 335pp.

A collection of 12 essays on the comparative analysis of deviance. Issues addressed include theoretical concerns and methodological problems of comparative research, juvenile delinquency and minority status, evolutionary and historical social control, crime measurement, economic crime, organized crime, and political crime. Features several cross-cultural essays.

059. Newman, Graeme R., and Franco Ferracuti (1980). "Introduction: The Limits and Possibilities of Comparative Criminology." Pp.7-16 in Graeme R. Newman (ed.), *Crime and Deviance: A Comparative Perspective*. Beverly Hills, California: Sage. Notes, bibliography.

Addresses the aims and importance of comparative criminology. Discusses the ongoing methodological and theoretical problems related to cross-cultural generalizations about crime, the relevance of historical comparative analysis, and the need for an international comparative framework.

060. Pinatel, Jean (1983). "International Society for Criminology." Pp.37-62 in vol.2 of Elmer H. Johnson (ed.) *International Handbook of Contemporary Developments in Criminology: General Issues and the Americas*. Westport, Connecticut: Greenwood Press. Bibliography.

Describes the nature and organizational functions of the International Society for Criminology. Focuses on its historical development, internal operations, and organizational agendas. Refers to various international governmental and nongovernmental organizations that are interested in the scholarly study of crime.

061. Reichel, Philip L. (1980). "Teaching About Crime in Communist Societies," *Teaching Sociology*, 7(2): 141-162. Notes, bibliography.

Introduces a methodological standard for teaching and evaluating student knowledge of socialist criminology. Includes a critique of communist-bloc theories of crime and repression of crime. Offers recommendations for a comparative analysis of Soviet and U.S. crime models.

062. Robertson, Roland, and Laurie Taylor (1973). *Deviance, Crime and Socio-Legal Control: Comparative Perspectives*. London: Martin Robertson. Notes, bibliography, 74pp.

Challenges the traditional preoccupation in criminology with the study of criminal law and the aetiology of crime. Outlines various approaches to comparative analysis. Reviews existing studies to demonstrate major conceptual and theoretical deficiencies in most comparative deviance and social control inquiries. Offers a comparative approach on deviance and social control relationships.

063. Robertson, Roland, and Laurie Taylor (1974). "Problems in the Comparative Analysis of Deviance: A Survey and A Proposal." Pp.91-123 in Paul Rockand Mary McIntosh (eds.), *Deviance and Social Control*. London: Tavistock. Notes, bibliography.

Assesses deficiencies in concepts, methods and theories of comparative deviance. Problems include premature comparative generalizations, objectivism, equivalency, and the use of official crime rates. Stresses the need for subjective and cultural integration in comparative research.

064. Rokkan, Stein, and Kazimierz Szczerba Likiernik (1968). "A Programme for the Advancement of Comparative Social Science Research: The Action of the International Social Science Council." Pp.1-13 in Stein Rokkan (ed.), *Comparative Research Across Cultures and Nations*. Paris: Mouton. Notes.

Introduces the main topics discussed at the Round Table Conference on Comparative Research held in Paris in April, 1965. Topics include the cross-cultural method, historical change, processes of modernization, aggregate statistical comparisons of nations, and sample surveys. Describes the International Social Science Council's role in the development and execution of conference programs.

065. Rokkan, Stein (ed.) (1968). *Comparative Research Across Cultures and Nations*. Paris: Mouton. Notes, bibliography, vi + 238pp.

This collection of 13 essays addresses various aspects of comparative analysis. These include the rationale for cross-cultural analysis, historical and developmental analysis, and quantitative procedures for cross-cultural comparisons. Refers to research in developed and developing nations.

066. Schwendinger, Herman, and Julia Schwendinger (1975). "Defenders of order or guardians of human rights?." Pp.113-146 in Ian Taylor, Paul Walton, and Jock Young (eds.), *Critical Criminology*. London: Routledge & Kegan Paul. Notes, references.

A widely read essay on the debate about the proper object of study for criminology. Rejects the legalistic definition and argues that the only possible definition of crime is one grounded in human rights discourse. As such, imperialism, sexism, and racism are crimes, as indeed are some exploitative social systems.

067. Schwirian, Kent P. (1973). "Some Analytical Problems in the Comparative Test of Ecological Theories." Pp.347-375 in Michael Armer and Allen D.Grimshaw (eds.), *Comparative Social Research:*

Methodological Problems and Strategies. New York: John Wiley. Bibliography.

Addresses methodological difficulties in comparative ecological analyses, designs, and theories. Difficulties include problems with comparability of community area and differences in scope of data inputs, variables, and models. Outlines the underlying methodological issues in factorial, distant gradient, sectorial models, and segregation models. Demonstrates problems of comparability in an ecological study conducted in Puerto Rico and Canada.

068. Sebba, Leslie (1979). "The Comparative Method in Criminology," *Israel Studies in Criminology*, 5: 15-36. Notes, bibliography.

Outlines five common comparative typologies in Israeli criminology. These include theoretical studies; analysis which refers to comparative data; the utilization of a research instrument developed in another country; the replication of a cross-cultural theory or hypothesis; and cross-cultural studies. Reviews comparative Israeli studies to exemplify the typologies. Briefly reviews methodological problems.

069. Seibel, Dieter S. (1972). "Social Deviance in Comparative Perspective." Pp.251-281 in Robert A. Scott and Jack D. Douglas (eds.), *Theoretical Perspectives on Deviance*. New York: Basic Books. Bibliography.

Investigates social deviance in complex and simple African societies including the Barotse, the Bantu states, and the Nuer. Examines relationships between social deviance and social integration. Discusses African group membership and the structure of social sanctions. Reviews various theories and previous research findings and offers some universal propositions deemed relevant to the theoretical study of deviance.

070. Shelley, Louise I. (ed.) (1981). *Readings in Comparative Criminology*. Carbondale, Illinois: Southern Illinois University Press. Notes, bibliography, xxxiv + 273pp.

Offers 13 essays that focus on issues relevant to comparative criminology, including theoretical analysis, methodology, and selected cross-cultural studies. Selections include gender, juvenile delinquency, homicide, crime trends, crime and economic development, and criminal justice.

071. Skocpol, Theda, and Margaret Somers (1980). "The Uses of Comparative History in Macrosocial Inquiry," *Comparative Studies in Society and History*, 22(2): 174-197. Notes.

An important theoretical outline of the three dominant logics of comparative historical analysis, including macro-causal analysis, contrast-oriented analysis, and parallel comparative history. Uses relevant data to exemplify each category and to discuss the relationship among macrosocial comparative research, research designs, and argument presentation. Discusses the strengths and limitations of each type.

072. Szabo, Denis (1975). "Comparative Criminology," *Journal of Criminal Law and Criminology*, 66(3): 366-379. Annotations.

An article prepared as part of a Festschrift for the Gluecks. Argues that comparative criminology has failed largely because of the rise of many national criminologies. Meanders through a variety of dominant criminological theories, especially interactionism, and concludes that comparative criminology will only advance by studying simple pre-industrial societies.

073. Tonry, Michael, and Norval Morris (eds.) (1983). *Crime and Justice: An Annual Review of Research*, vol. 5, Chicago: University of Chicago Press. Bibliographies, x + 310pp.

The second half of this volume consists of five single culture articles whose focus is the organizational features of criminological research in Australia, Canada, Great Britain, The Netherlands, and the Federal Republic of Germany.

074. Walton, John (1973). "Standardized Case Comparison: Observations on Method in Comparative Sociology." Pp.173-191 in Michael Armer and Allen D. Grimshaw (eds.), *Comparative Social Research: Methodological Problems and Strategies*. New York: John Wiley. Notes, bibliography.

Focuses on the vast methodological difficulties in comparative analysis and the need for a rigorous comparative sociological method. Assesses three comparative methods: comparative case studies, comparative analysis of archival data, and standardized case comparison. Proposes and illustrates a methodological framework for comparative analysis.

075. West, W. Gordon (1989). "Towards a Global Criminal Justice Problematic," *Journal of Human Justice*, 1(1): 99-112. Bibliography.

Argues that most comparative criminology is flawed in its basic assumptions and perspectives. A critical comparative criminology, instead, should be based on a world systems model, and have human rights as one of its primary objectives. Suggests how Marxist concepts such as 'reproduction', 'production', 'the state', and 'transformation' can profitably be applied to Canadian crime and justice.

076. Wiarda, Howard J. (1981) "The Ethnocentrism of the Social Sciences: Implications for Research and Policy," *The Review of Politics*, 43(2): 163-197. Bibliography.

Seriously challenges the view that the research methods and theoretical generalizations of western social science have universal relevance. Discussion addresses the inherent nature of western ethnocentrism, its political and social consequences, and its developing theoretical imposition on Third World nations.

077. Wolfgang, Marvin E. (ed.) (1968). *Crime and Culture: Essays in Honor of Thorsten Sellin*. New York: John Wiley. Notes, references, appendix, biographies, xv + 462pp.

Twenty-one essays in honor of Thorsten Sellin. Anthology focuses on various aspects of criminology, including the state of the field, theory, measurement and criminal statistics, empirical research, historical penology, and contemporary corrections. Several of the essays are explicitly comparative in scope.

2

Cross-National Data

078. Ali, Badr-El-Din (1986). Methodological Problems in International Criminal Justice Research," *International Journal of Comparative and Applied Criminal Justice*,10(2): 163-176. Notes, bibliography, appendices.

Discusses numerous methodological obstacles in comparative criminal justice research. Focuses on areas of incompatibility, including problems related to the cultural definition and meaning of crime, language, values, socio-political variation, and reporting and measurement consistency. Addresses the importance of validity in comparative analysis. Author discusses problems he encountered during analysis of a pilot study of 35 nations.

079. Anson, Richard H., and James N. Cole (1981). "On Structural Effects in Criminal Justice Research," *International Journal of Comparative and Applied Criminal Justice*, 5(2): 213-219. Bibliography.

Outlines the methodological and philosophical inconsistencies in comparative organizational behavioral studies. Discusses inadequate sampling designs, measurement difficulties, and the need for interorganizational understanding and synchronized testing.

080. Archer, Dane, and Rosemary Gartner (1984). *Violence and Crime in Cross-National Perspective*. New Haven, Connecticut: Yale University Press. Bibliography, ix + 341pp.

A widely-acclaimed work whose focus is the development of the Comparative Crime Data File ('CCDF'). The CCDF (pp.171-328) lists the crime rates of 110 societies and 44 major cities from 1900 to 1970. Crimes include murder, manslaughter, homicide, rape, assault, robbery, and theft. Authors explain the history of the CCDF, its concepts, methodology, and limitations. Includes three chapters that address the respective effects on homicide of war, city size, and the death penalty. [See also #s 142,143,144,145, and Appendix A].

081. Armer, Michael (1973). "Methodological Problems and Possibilities in Comparative Research." Pp.49-79 in Michael Armer and Allen D. Grimshaw (eds.), *Comparative Social Research: Methodological Problems and Strategies.* New York: John Wiley. Notes, bibliography.

Outlines major differences between comparative and noncomparative research. Discusses essential methodological issues of comparative research. Methodological difficulties include variations in concepts, language, meaning, and socio-cultural conditions.

082. Bennett, Richard R. (1989). *Correlates of Crime: A Study of Nations, 1960-1984.* Ann Arbor, Michigan: Interuniversity Consortium for Political and Social Research. ICPSR No. 9258. Documentation has tables, appendices, supporting bibliography, 36pp.

Correlates of Crime ('COC') is a sequential data archive file with data on 52 nations from 1960 to 1984. Crimes include homicide, major and minor theft, fraud, and counterfeiting. Nations are from all major world regions. National data include offense and offender characteristics, and national social, political and economic information. Data drawn *inter alia* from Interpol, United Nations, World Bank, International Labour Organization, and International Monetary Fund. COC Data set available on ICPSR diskettes. [See also Appendix A].

083. Bennett, Richard R., and Louise Shelley (1985). "Criminalité et développement économique: Une analyse internationale longitudinale," *Annales de Vacresson*, 22:13-31. Bibliography, appendices.

Compares the relationship between social and economic development and variations in the crime trends of industrialized and developing nations from 1962 to 1978. Utilizes a longitudinal design with Interpol data.

084. Bennett, Richard R., and James P. Lynch (1990). "Does a Difference Make a Difference? Comparing Cross-National Crime Indicators," *Criminology*, 28(1): 153-182. Bibliography.

Compares the reliability of four widely-used data sets for descriptive, cross-sectional, and longitudinal studies. Data sets are provided by Interpol, the Comparative Crime Data File, the United Nations, and the World Health Organization. Data set attributes include scope, crime definitions, quality control, source, coverage, and period. Concludes that differences in the data sets do not for most explanatory purposes affect comparative generalizations about crime rates.

085. Blazicek, Donald L. and Galan Janeksela (1978). "Some Comments on Comparative Methodologies in Criminal Justice," *International Journal of Criminology and Penology*, 6(3): 233-245. Notes, bibliography.

Outlines standard social scientific research procedures in comparative criminology and the importance of the comparative research method for adequate theory construction. Describes commonplace comparative methodological problems and errors, with emphasis on criminal justice research. Offers suggestions for comparative research.

086. Block, Richard (1983). "A Comparison of National Crime Surveys." *World Congress of Criminology*, Vienna. Bibliography, 40pp.

Outlines variations in method and content of 8 national crime surveys conducted in the U.S., The Netherlands, Australia, Sweden, Israel, England and Wales, Scotland, and Canada. Includes sample and questionnaire designs, demographic variables, victimization data, and theoretical analysis. Crimes include rape, assault/battery, sexual molestation, robbery, burglary/breaking and entering, motor vehicle theft, theft from auto, bicycle theft, pickpocketing, simple theft, vandalism, and fraud. Compares incident information, attitudes, and behavior.

087. Block, Richard (1984). "The Impact of Victimization, rates and patterns: A Comparison of the Netherlands and the United States." Pp.23-49 in Richard Block (ed.) *Victimization and Fear of Crime*. Washington, D.C.: U.S. Department of Justice, NCJ-93872. Bibliography.

Uses Dutch (1977) and U.S. (1976) National Crime Surveys to compare victimization patterns in The Netherlands and the U.S. Crimes include completed house burglaries, assaults, robberies, and theft. Features methodological design, crime index, socio-economic and gender characteristics and analysis of crime patterns. Discusses variations in victimization rates for both countries.

088. Braithwaite, John, and David Biles (1980). "Crime Victimization in Australia: A Comparison with the U.S.," *Journal of Crime and Justice*, 3: 95-110. Notes, bibliography.

Compares 1974-1975 Australian and 1975 U.S. National Crime Survey findings for the crimes of breaking and entering, theft, motor vehicle theft, fraud, forgery and false pretenses, rape and attempted rape, robbery, and assault. Discusses methodological and definitional comparability. Compares victimization findings with those of official crime statistics.

089. Breen, Richard, and David B. Rottman (1985). *Crime Victimization in the Republic of Ireland*. Dublin: Economic and Social Research Institute. Paper No.121. Bibliography, appendices, 119 pp.

The first Irish victimization survey. Discusses the methodology and uses of victimization surveys, the level of criminal victimization, and victimological risk analysis. Ch.4 ('Irish Crime Levels in Comparative Context', pp.54-70) compares Irish crime rates in the period 1950-1979 with those in the U.S., Canada, Holland, England and Wales, and Scotland. Concludes with recommendations for crime policy, crime statistics, and criminological research.

090. Buchholz, Erich (1987). "Reasons for the Low Rate of Crime in the German Democratic Republic," *Crime and Social Justice*, 29: 26-42. Notes, bibliography.

Contrasts official crime rates in the Federal Republic of Germany and the German Democratic Republic. Provides aggregate crime rates for a variety of crimes between 1946 and 1984. Discusses the effects of the social, ideological, political, and economic environments on criminal etiology. Discusses methodological difficulties.

091. Clinard, Marshall B. (1978). "Comparative Crime Victimization Surveys: Some Problems and Results," *International Journal of Criminology and Penology*, 6(3): 221-231. Notes, bibliography.

Focuses on the problems of conducting and comparing victimization surveys and official crime statistics, particularly in cross-cultural analysis. Discusses the development of comparative criminology, the unreliability of official statistics, and the many difficulties in victimization research and cross-cultural comparison. Outlines alternative victimization research methods for comparative research, theft insurance data, hospital statistics, and crime victimization surveys.

092. Elder, Joseph W. (1973). "Problems of Cross-Cultural Methodology: Instrumentation and Interviewing in India." Pp.119-148 in Michael Armer and Allen D. Grimshaw (eds.), *Comparative Social Research: Methodological Problems and Strategies*. New York: John Wiley. Notes, bibliography.

Identifies author's methodological difficulties during research in two areas of India in 1963. Outlines cross-cultural variations in language, economics, caste hierarchies, and customs. Discusses the methodological issues relating to the understanding of intrasocietal and intersocietal diversity and systematic differentiation, and questions comparability.

093. Form, William H. (1973). "Field Problems in Comparative Research: The Politics of Distrust." Pp.83-117 in Michael Armer and Allen D. Grimshaw (eds.), *Comparative Social Research: Methodological Problems and Strategies*. New York: John Wiley. Notes, bibliography.

Reviews various problems of respondent cooperation encountered during author's field research in the U.S., Mexico, Argentina, India, and Italy from 1948 to 1969. Problems include bureaucratic distrust, social conflict, and political ideology. Offers impressions for future researchers.

094. Friday, Paul C. and Subhash R. Sonnad (1979). "Respondents and Non-Respondents in Survey Research: The Offender Sample," *International Journal of Comparative and Applied Criminal Justice*, 3(1): 35-42. Bibliography.

Utilizes Swedish data to examine cross-cultural differences between survey respondents and non-respondents. Describes methodology and findings, and provides a theoretical discussion of respondent and non-respondent variance in survey research. Includes a review of relevant literature.

095. Frey, Frederick W. (1970). "Cross-Cultural Survey Research in Political Science." Pp.173-294 in Robert T. Holt and John E. Turner (eds.), *The Methodology of Comparative Research*. New York: The Free Press. Notes.

Discusses the purposes of cross-cultural survey research, and identifies various conceptual and structural difficulties found in cross-cultural survey research. Distinguishes cross-cultural surveys from other forms of survey investigation conducted by political scientists.

096. Gurr, Ted Robert (1977). "Crime Trends in Modern Democracies Since 1945," *Annales internationales de criminologie*, 16(1-2): 41-85. Notes, bibliography.

A cross-cultural comparison of common crime trends in economically developed western democracies from 1945 to 1975. Crimes include murder and manslaughter, assault, robbery, burglary, larceny/petty theft, white-collar crime, sexual and moral offenses, and public order offenses. Utilizes official crime data for each country. Outlines comparative statistical data and discusses methodological design, legal aspects, crime and conviction rates, and findings. [See also Appendix A].

097. Huang, W.S. Wilson, and Charles F. Wellford (1989). "Assessing Indicators of Crime Among International Crime Data Series," *Criminal Justice Policy Review*, 3(1): 28-48. Notes, bibliography.

Compares data series (1970 and 1980) to test classification equivalence in official reporting of murder, robbery, theft, homicide, assault, and sex offenses. Countries include Sweden, Denmark, Norway, Australia, England and Wales, Italy, Poland, New Zealand, Syria, West Germany, Switzerland, and the U.S. Employs several crime data sources, including Interpol [see # 098], the United Nations Crime Survey [see # 109], the World Health Organization [see Appendix A], the Comparative Crime Data File [see Appendix A], and Gurr's [see # 096] longitudinal data. Reviews methodological problems of crime definitions and meaning. Findings and research proposals provided.

098. Interpol. (1951 -). *International Crime Statistics*. Paris: International Criminal Police Organization.

A very limited set of crime data that is assembled by the General Secretariat of the International Criminal Police Organization. The volumes appear sporadically, and the accuracy of the crime data in them is highly questionable. Crimes reported include murder, sex offenses, larceny, fraud, counterfeiting, and drug offenses.

099. Kalish, Carol B. (1988). *International Crime Rates*. Bureau of Justice Statistics, U.S. Department of Justice, NCJ-110776. Appendix, 11pp.

Report utilizes crime data collected from the United Nations, Interpol, and the World Health Organization. Identifies and compares international crime rates for 1980-1984. Examines homicide, rape, robbery, burglary, theft, and auto theft in 41 countries. Discusses problems with comparability of different data sources and outlines crime definitions used.

100. Kennedy, Leslie W., and David R. Forder (1990). "Routine Activities and Crime: An Analysis of Victimization in Canada," *Criminology*, 28(1): 137-152. Notes, bibliography.

Finds that for violent crimes in Canada there are strong interaction effects between victims' demographic characteristics and routine activities that occur at night and away from home. Uses 1984 Canadian Urban Victimization Survey to dispute findings from U.S. data. Victimization is contingent on the exposure that comes from following certain lifestyles.

101. Krohn, Marvin, and Charles Wellford (1977). "A Static and Dynamic Analysis of Crime and the Primary Dimensions of Nations," *International Journal of Criminology and Penology*, 5(1): 1-16. Notes, bibliography.

Examines the relationship between variables alleged to be important in social change and crime index analysis, which is identified as one aspect of social disorganization. Utilizes Interpol data and World Handbook of Social and Political Indicators as independent variables, and changing homicide, property, and overall crime rates in 96 countries as dependent variables. Reviews previous comparative research. Discusses methodological design and comparative findings.

102. Martin, John M., Anne T. Romano, and James F. Haran (1988). "International Crime Patterns: Challenges to Traditional Criminological Theory and Research," *Criminal Justice Research Bulletin*, 4(2): 1-8. Bibliography.

Addresses the need to investigate the international crime patterns of espionage, terrorism, arms trafficking, and drug trafficking. Examines the theoretical neglect of various international crimes. Discusses contemporary preoccupation with traditional crime analysis and includes a brief review of relevant literature.

103. Newman, Graeme R. (1977). "Problems of Method in Comparative Criminology," *International Journal of Comparative and Applied Criminal Justice*, 1(1): 17-31. Bibliography.

Reviews various methodological obstacles to comparative criminology, especially the problem of comparability. Obstacles include value differences in legal concepts and legal systems; interview data, meaning, and temporal equivalence; and organizational and sampling problems. Reviews comparative literature.

104. Rokkan, Stein, and Sidney Verba. (1969). *Comparative Survey Analysis*. Paris: Mouton. Bibliography, xiv + 343pp.

Offers various strategies and uses for survey analysis. Part 1 outlines historical origins; trends; structural research characteristics of survey analysis; the application of survey research in comparative political analysis; and cross-cultural difficulties in survey research. Part 2 offers an annotated bibliography of survey research literature.

105. Scheuch, Erwin K. (1968). "The Cross-Cultural Use of Sample Surveys: Problems of Comparability." Pp.176-209 in Stein Rokkan (ed.), *Comparative Research Across Cultures and Nations*. Paris: Mouton. Bibliographies.

Focuses on the problem of comparability and outlines basic methodological and conceptual difficulties in cross-cultural sample surveys. Difficulties include variations in meaning, language and concept barriers, and questionnaire techniques which ignore cultural diversity. Offers suggestions for enhancing comparability.

106. Sellin, Thorsten (1967). "International Criminal Statistics," *Criminology*, 5(2): 2-11. Notes.

Historically reviews the aim and establishment of the first national (1825 in France) and international (1829) system of criminal statistics. Discusses the methodological deficiencies of official crime measurements -- e.g., the Uniform Crime Reports -- which hinder reliable comparative analysis. Offers suggestions for the international implementation of criminal classification.

107. Sellin, Thorsten, and Marvin E. Wolfgang (1964). *The Measurement of Delinquency*. New York: John Wiley. Notes, appendices, x + 423pp.

Examines qualitative and quantitative juvenile delinquency data in Philadelphia, Pennsylvania, in order to develop a scale from which crime seriousness can be indexed and measured independently of legal labels. Discussion of methodological framework and subsequent measurement features historical, official, and social cohort data. Provides a detailed outline and interpretation of the theoretical and procedural functions of research design.

108. Teske, Raymond H.C. and Harald R. Arnold (1982). "Comparison of the Criminal Statistics of the United States and the Federal Republic of Germany," *Journal of Criminal Justice*, 10: 359-374. Notes, bibliography.

Recognizes the difficulty of comparing cross-national crime rates. Devises a method, based on the categories of the Uniform Crime Reports, for comparing U.S. crime rates (sample is Texas) with those in the Federal Republic of Germany. Translates articles from the latter's penal code.

109. United Nations (1981). "United Nations Crime Survey." Pp.153-174 in Louise I. Shelley (ed.), *Readings in Comparative Criminology*. Carbondale, Illinois: Southern Illinois University Press. Notes.

Reports findings of a 1977 cross-cultural analysis of international crime problems and the administration of justice. Utilizes government survey data from many nations. Outlines crime rates worldwide and for developed and developing countries from 1970 to 1975. Crimes include intentional homicide, assault, sex crimes, kidnapping, robbery, theft, fraud, illegal traffic in drugs, and drug and alcohol abuse. Describes crime prevention and control methods and their geographical variation.

110. Van Dijk, Jan J.M., Pat Mayhew, and Martin Killias (1990). *Experiences of Crime across the World: Key findings from the 1989 International Crime Survey*. Deventer and Boston: Kluwer. Notes, annexes, bibliography, ix + 188pp.

Reports on a large victimization survey conducted on adults in Australia, Belgium, Canada, England and Wales, Federal Republic of Germany, Finland, France, The Netherlands, Northern Ireland, Norway, Scotland, Spain, Switzerland, and the U.S. Local surveys also conducted in Poland, Indonesia, and Japan. Victimization rates reported include assault, automobile theft, burglary, robbery, theft, and sexual offenses. Examines cross-national differences in crime rates, responses to crime, and crime prevention measures.

111. Verkko, Veli (1956). "Survey of Current Practice in Criminal Statistics." Pp.5-33 in vol.3 of *Transactions of the Westermarck Society*. Copenhagen: Ejnar Munksgaard. Notes.

Outlines essential classification features, limitations, and uses of official police, judicial, and prisoner statistics. Refers to statistical publications in Finland, Sweden, Norway, Denmark, Germany, England and Wales, Northern Ireland, Scotland, Canada, The Netherlands, the U.S., and Belgium.

112. Vetere, Eduardo, and Graeme Newman (1977). "International Crime Statistics: An Overview from a Comparative Perspective," *Criminology and Penology Abstracts*, 17(3): 251-273. Annexes, bibliography.

Reviews international attempts to develop methodological procedures for the construction of cross-national crime statistics. Organizations examined include the United Nations, Interpol, the Council of Europe, and the Organization of Economic Cooperation and Development. Discusses methodological problems of official crime statistics and their utilization. Offers proposals for enhancement of data comparability. Annex provides prison population rates for many countries from 1972 to 1974.

113. Vigderhous, Gideon (1978). "Methodological Problems Confronting Cross-Cultural Criminological Research Using Official Data," *Human Relations*, 31(3): 229-247. Notes, bibliography.

Explores the problem of cross-cultural comparability in the context of official statistics of homicide rates. Uses World Health Organization data. Suggests that the question of reliability should be presented at an empirical level rather than at the level of general concepts.

114. Wilkins, Leslie T. (1980). "World Crime: To Measure or Not to Measure?" Pp.17-41 in Graeme R. Newman (ed.), *Crime and Deviance: A Comparative Perspective*. Beverly Hills, California: Sage. Notes, bibliography.

Provides a compelling argument for a reconceptualization of comparative criminology and the use of official cross-national data. Focuses on the importance of comparative analysis, its historical roots, conceptual and methodological difficulties, cultural distinctions, and proposes a theoretical framework for future investigation.

115. Wolfgang, Marvin E. (1967). "International Criminal Statistics: A Proposal," *Journal of Criminal Law, Criminology and Police Science*, 58(1): 65-69. Notes.

A brief but influential essay that explicitly addresses the problem of cross-cultural variation in legal definitions of crime and in the seriousness of crime. Proposes a weighted method for collecting cross-national crime statistics on offenses against persons and against property yet which respects cultural diversity.

116. World Health Organization (1921-). "Homicide Statistics," In *World Health Statistics Annual/Annuaire de statistiques sanitaires mondiales*. Geneva: World Health Organization.

Reports based on death certificates are sent in voluntarily by member countries. Reports published since 1921. Three age-specific and sex-specific entries refer to 'suicide and self-inflicted injury,' 'homicide and injury purposely inflicted by other persons,' and 'other violence.' [See also Appendix A].

3

Perceptions of Crime

117. Arzt, Gunther (1979). "Responses to the Growth of Crime in the United States and West Germany: A Comparison of Changes in Criminal Law and Societal Attitudes," *Cornell International Law Journal*, 12(1): 43-64. Notes.

Compares the legal and societal reaction to rising crime rates in the U.S. and West Germany. Reviews official crime rate differences for rape, burglary, and robbery in 1976. Discusses changes in official and unofficial responses to crime in both countries and in legal doctrine.

118. Bell, Wendell and Robert V. Robinson (1978). "An Index of Evaluated Equality: Measuring Conceptions of Social Justice in England and the United States," *Comparative Studies in Sociology: An Annual Compilation of Research* (ed. Richard F. Tomasson, Greenwich, Connecticut: JAI Press), 1: 235-270. Notes, bibliography, appendices.

Uses an empirical procedure to evaluate social equality and conceptions of social justice. Tests this method by comparing social justice in England and the U.S. Discusses the meaningful relationship between concepts of justice and societal inequality. Discusses methodological design, index reliability, efficacy, and findings.

119. Bloom, Alfred H. (1977). "A Cognitive Dimension of Social Control: The Hong Kong Chinese in Cross-Cultural Perspective," Pp.67-81 in Amy Auerbacher Wilson, Sidney Greenblatt, and Richard Whittingham Wilson (eds.), *Deviance and Social Control in Chinese Society*. New York: Praeger. Annotations.

Compares the relationship between cognitive processes and structural and political dimensions of social control in China, France, and the U.S. Findings from culturally-sensitive questionnaires suggest a cognitive relationship between social beliefs and structural and political thought processes as forms of social control.

120. Connor, Walter D. (1970). "Deviant Behavior in Capitalist Society - The Soviet Image," *Journal of Criminal Law, Criminology and Police Science*, 61(4): 554-564. Notes.

Discusses Soviet concepts of deviance in capitalist societies and how deviance is held to be directly related to the structural forces and bourgeois ideology of capitalism. Includes descriptions of Soviet analyses of crime. Questions the purpose and utility of Soviet analysis of the causes of deviant behavior in capitalist societies.

121. Evans, Sandra S., and Joseph E. Scott (1984). "The Seriousness of Crime Cross-Culturally: The Impact of Religiosity," *Criminology*, 22(1): 39-59. Notes, bibliography.

Utilizes survey data from the U.S. and the Middle East to assess the perceptual seriousness of various crimes and sanctions in a comparative context. Also employs religious sentiments to examine perceived seriousness of crimes. Compares the two measurement procedures. Discusses research findings and implications.

122. Goodman, Nancy (1967). *Yugoslavia -- A New Look At Crime*. London: Institute for the Study and Treatment of Delinquency. Appendix, 40pp.

This brief report is the result of a 19-day study tour of Yugoslavia by a group of English students in 1966. Focuses on Yugoslavia's legal, judicial, educational, and welfare systems and offender treatment. Discusses essential systematic differences in social and political philosophies between Yugoslavia and the United Kingdom.

123. Hollander, Paul (ed.) (1969). *American and Soviet Society: A Reader in Comparative Sociology and Perception*. Englewood Cliffs, New Jersey: Prentice-Hall. Notes, xviii + 589pp.

A collection of 94 short comparative essays focusing on a variety of dominant institutional and sociological aspects of U.S. and Soviet societies. Part 5 ('Social Problems') reprints essays by leading U.S. and Soviet scholars on juvenile delinquency.

124. Lipset, Seymour Martin (1963). "The Value Patterns of Democracy: A Case Study in Comparative Analysis," *American Sociological Review*, 28(4): 515-531. Notes.

Employs achievement-ascription, universalism-particularism and specificity-diffuseness as pattern variables to compare national values in the democratic nations of the U.S., England, Canada, and Australia. Analyses those institutions which are associated with the state. Discusses cross-cultural variations in value patterns.

125. Newman, Graeme R. (1975). "Toward a Transnational Classification of Crime and Deviance," *Journal of Cross-Cultural Psychology*, 6(3): 297-315. Notes, bibliography, appendices.

Employs a framework termed 'Norm Resistance Scale' to compare several aspects of the perception of robbery, incest, white-collar crime, homosexuality, abortion, drugs, environmental pollution, negligence, and public protest. Countries include the U.S., Yugoslavia, Sardinia (Italy), Iran and Indonesia. Outlines methodological design, including urban/rural sample description and perceptual aspects measured. Findings interpreted and discussed.

126. Newman, Graeme R. (1976). *Comparative Deviance: Perception and Law in Six Cultures.* New York: Elsevier. Notes, bibliographies, xii + 332pp.

Uses questionnaire data to examine public responses in 6 countries to legal perceptions of robbery, incest, homosexuality, abortion, factory pollution, public protest against government policy, appropriation of government funds for personal use, and drug use. Countries include India, Indonesia, Iran, Italy (Sardinia), Yugoslavia, and the U.S. Findings outline variation and similarity in cross-cultural responses. Methodological design discussed.

127. Normandeau, André (1966). "The Measurement of Delinquency in Montreal," *Journal of Criminal Law, Criminology and Police Science*, 57(2): 172-177. Notes.

Employs Sellin and Wolfgang's methodological index model to compare the perceived seriousness of 15 offenses in Montreal, Canada and Philadelphia, Pennsylvania. Briefly discusses research design, finding of partial replication, and impressions.

128. Opolot, James S.E. (1982). "Contributions of the African Novel to the Development of African Criminology," *International Journal of Comparative and Applied Criminal Justice*, 6(2): 203-211. Bibliography.

Describes how African novels encourage the development of themes in contemporary African criminology. Identifies various pre-independence, colonial, and post-colonial literary themes which portray a collective social and political voice.

129. Osgood, Charles E. (1967). "On the Strategy of Cross-National Research into Subjective Culture," *Social Science Information*, 6(1): 5-37. Bibliography.

Exemplifies three comparative studies to address various methodological and conceptual difficulties of cross-cultural analysis. Focuses on problems of cultural subjectivity, e.g., language, interpretation, and meaning. Outlines cross-cultural design and offers procedural suggestions and impressions.

130. Perkins, H. Wesley, and Wendell Bell (1980). "Alienation and Social Justice in England and the United States: The Polity and Economy," *Comparative Social Research* (ed. Richard F. Tomasson, Greenwich, Connecticut: JAI Press), 3: 71-101. Bibliography, appendix.

Employs various theories to introduce a model for interpreting political alienation and its causal relationship with administrative and economic institutions in England and the U.S. Discusses methodological and theoretical aspects of the study.

131. Scott, Joseph E., and Fahad Al-Thakeb (1977). "The Public's Perception of Crime: Scandinavia, West Europe, the Middle East, and the United States." Pp.78-88 in C. Ronald Huff (ed.),

Contemporary Corrections. Beverly Hills, California: Sage. Notes, appendix.

Examines the relationship between public perceptions of crime and punishment in Finland, Sweden, Denmark, The Netherlands, and Britain. Uses 1974 questionnaire data to measure perceptions of social harm and moral indignation for 24 crimes, including 7 U.S. Index Crimes, 8 white-collar crimes, 3 public order violations, 4 drug-related crimes, and 2 unidentified crimes. Provides demographic and incarceration data.

132. Scott, Joseph E., and Fahad Al-Thakeb (1980). "Perceptions of Deviance Cross-Culturally." Pp.42-67 in Graeme R. Newman (ed.), *Crime and Deviance: A Comparative Perspective*. Beverly Hills, California: Sage. Bibliography.

Utilizes data from the U.S., England, Finland, Sweden, Norway, Denmark, The Netherlands, and Kuwait in order to classify consensual perceptions of crime seriousness and of sanctions for murder, rape, robbery, and assault. Examines comparative literature on crime perceptions and the relationships among social ideology, crime definitions, reporting practices, and official statistics. Reviews research findings from the U.S., Western Europe, and the Middle East. [See also # 131].

133. Skovron, Sandra Evans, Joseph E. Scott, and P. Kamalakara Rao (1987). "Cross-Cultural Perceptions of Offense Severity: The United States, India and Kuwait," *International Journal of Comparative and Applied Criminal Justice*, 11(1): 47-60. Notes, bibliography.

Measures and compares perceptions of the seriousness of 37 crimes and 17 sanctions in the U.S., India, and Kuwait. Includes cross-cultural research review. Describes methodological features and limitations. Findings outline cross-cultural differences. Theoretical discussion and indications provided.

134. Talbot, Charles K. (1982). "The Moral Mirror Image of Crime: A Comparison of Recorded Crime and Crime Recorded in Fiction." *International Journal of Comparative and Applied Criminal Justice*, 6(2): 195-202. Bibliography.

Explores the relationship between crime which is reported in fictional literature and officially recorded crime statistics. Uses New York Times Book Review (1979 and 1981) and Canadian crime statistics (for Ontario, 1979-1980). Details methodological design and findings inferring negative quantitative and qualitative correlations. Reviews moral and ethical implications.

135. Teske, Raymond H.C., and Harald R. Arnold (1987). "A Comparative Analysis of Factors Related to Fear of Crime in the United States (Texas) and the Federal Republic of Germany (Baden-Württemberg)," *International Journal of Comparative and Applied Criminal Justice*, 11(1): 33-45. Notes, bibliography.

Based on a victimization survey testing whether the same factors predict the fear of crime in both societies. Sex, community size, perception of the crime problem, and perceived effectiveness of local police accounted for 20.2% of the variation in the U.S. and 24.4% in the F.R.G. in the fear of walking alone within one mile of one's home at night; the same variables, plus family income, accounted for 16.1% of the variation in the U.S. and 10.8% in the F.R.G. in the fear of walking alone within one block of one's home at night.

136. Van Kerckvoorde, Jaak, Lode Walgrave, Hanna Malewska, and Vincent Peyre (1985). "Evaluation by Professionals of the Seriousness of Juvenile Delinquency: With a Belgian-French-Polish Comparison," *Annales de Vaucresson*, 1(22):110-125. Bibliography, appendix.

Compares the attitudes of juvenile justice professionals toward youth offenses in Belgium, France, and Poland. Describes methodology, comparative difficulties, and findings.

137. Yuen, Gwenson (1988). "A Cross-Cultural Perspective to Juvenile Offenders in the U.S.: A Chinese Perspective," *International Journal of Comparative and Applied Criminal Justice*, 12(1): 89-94. Bibliography.

Discusses ethnic and familial values of Chinese Americans. Demonstrates the need for judicial and professional sensitivity to cultural diversity. Stresses importance of ethnic socialization patterns, group assimilation and individuation, and meaningful communication among diverse ethnic groups. Briefly discusses previous cross-cultural studies on the universal quality of juveniles' perceptions of laws and rules

PART II

CROSS-NATIONAL CRIME RATES

4

Violent Crime

138. Abel, Ernest (ed.) (1987). *Homicide: a Bibliography.* Westport, Connecticut: Greenwood Press. xiii + 169pp.

A bibliography of homicide. Most, but not all, of the entries refer to single-culture studies of homicide.

139. Amnesty International (1989). *Amnesty International Report 1989.* Amnesty International USA: New York. Pp.316.

The 1989 edition of an annual series of Amnesty reports. This edition examines Amnesty International's work in 133 countries during 1988. Topics include prisoners of conscience, the denial of fair trials, victims of torture and disappearance, and executions. [See also Appendix D].

140. Andenaes, Johannes (1968). "Negligent Homicide in Some European Countries -- A Comparative Study." Pp.221-244 in Marvin E. Wolfgang (ed.), *Crime and Culture: Essays in Honor of Thorsten Sellin.* New York: John Wiley. Annotations.

Uses official homicide conviction statistics, especially for traffic fatalities, to investigate the relationship between negligent homicide and social status and judicial practice in Denmark, Finland, Norway, and Sweden. Comparisons made with Germany, France, and England. Methodological framework and findings discussed. New penal provisions suggested.

141. Archer, Dane, and Rosemary Gartner (1976). "Violent Acts and Violent Times: A Comparative Approach to Postwar Homicide Rates," *American Sociological Review*, 41(6): 937-963. Bibliography.

Uses Comparative Crime Data File to examine postwar homicide rates for numerous countries, and compares rate differences between 50 countries that experienced war and 30 that did not. Findings suggest that nations which experience war register postwar increases in homicide rates. Categorizes seven theories to interpret changing homicide rates.

142. Archer, Dane, and Rosemary Gartner (1977). "Homicide in 110 Nations: The Development of the Comparative Crime Data File," *Annales internationales de criminologie*, 16(1-2): 109-139. Bibliography.

Outlines the construction of a systematic historical crime data file (the Comparative Crime Data File) focusing on criminal homicide for the purpose of advancing international comparative research. Offers methodological observations on different homicide indicators, cross-sectional and longitudinal analyses of homicide in 100 societies, and urban and non-urban homicide rates over time.

143. Archer, Dane, and Rosemary Gartner (1978). "Legal Homicide and Its Consequences." Pp.219-232 in Irwin L. Kutash, Samuel B. Kutash, and Louis B. Schlesinger (eds.), *Violence: Perspectives on Murder and Aggresssion*. San Francisco, California: Jossey-Bass. Bibliography.

Examines homicide rate changes in combatant and control nations after World War I, World War II, the Vietnam War, and eleven other wars. Uses the 110-nation Comparative Crime Data File. A majority of combatant nations were found to experience post-war homicide rate increases of at least 10%; a majority of non-combatant nations experienced post-war homicide rate decreases of at least 10%.

144. Archer, Dane, and Rosemary Gartner (1981). "Peacetime Casualties: The Effects of War on the Violent Behavior of Noncombatants." Pp.215-226 in Elliot Aronson (ed.), *Readings About the Social Animal*. San Francisco, California: W.H. Freeman. Bibliography.

Utilizes the Comparative Crime Data File to investigate the relationship between state violence and increased personal violent behavior. Examines cross-cultural homicide rate changes for many combatant and controlled noncombatant countries. Findings suggest a relationship between warring nations and rising postwar homicide rates.

145. Archer, Dane, Rosemary Gartner, Robin Akert, and Tim Lockwood (1978). "Cities and Homicide: A New Look at an Old Paradox," *Comparative Studies in Sociology: An Annual Compilation of Research* (ed. Richard F. Tomasson, Greenwich, Connecticut: JAI Press), 1: 73-95. Notes, bibliography.

Examines the relationship between urbanism and violent crime. Utilizes homicide data in the Uniform Crime Reports and the Comparative Crime Data File to compare national and cross-national homicide rates for various cities. Discusses methodology and reviews relevant literature. Findings suggest a positive relationship between homicide and urbanism for larger rather than smaller cities. Provides demographic correlation data for homicide in 34 countries.

146. Bassiouni, M. Cherif (ed.) (1975). *International Terrorism and Political Crimes*. Springfield, Illinois: Charles C. Thomas. Notes, bibliography, appendices, xxvi + 594pp.

A collection of 31 papers presented at an international symposium in Italy in June 1973. Focuses on the prevention and abolition of political crimes and international terrorism. Appendices discuss international law proposals, including the prevention and punishment of terrorism, protection of U.S. diplomatic personnel, chronology of terrorist incidents involving foreign personnel, and suggestions for an international definition of terrorism.

147. Bohannan, Paul (1969). "Cross-Cultural Comparison of Aggression and Violence." Pp.1189-1239 in Donald J. Mulvihill and Melvin M. Tumin (eds.), *Crimes of Violence*, vol. 13. Washington, D.C.: U.S. Government Printing Office. Bibliography.

Investigates several important aspects of violence and aggression. These include variations among violence, aggression, and emotions; the relationships among diverse social groups, social structure, and forms of violence; and the relationships among cultural attitudes, cognitive learning, and violent and warlike behavior. Provides comparative examples in Italy, medieval Europe, New Guinea, North American Indians, and the U.S.

148. Chappell, Duncan (1976). "Cross-Cultural Research on Forcible Rape," *International Journal of Criminology and Penology*, 4(3): 295-304. Notes, bibliography.

Reviews cross-cultural research studies of rape. Addresses various difficulties in comparative analysis, e.g., variation in national legal definitions and their social and cultural determinants and interpretation. Offers recommendations for future comparative rape analysis, including intensive research by historians and anthropologists, and the use of anthropological data and an ethnological approach.

149. Colijn, Jan G., David Lester, and A. Slothouwer (1985). "Firearms and Crime in the Netherlands: A Comparison with the United States of America," *International Journal of Comparative and Applied Criminal Justice*, 9(1): 49-55. Bibliography.

Investigates firearm legislation and ownership and their relationship with crime in The Netherlands and the U.S. Discusses gun ownership legislation, the relationship between gun ownership and crime incidence, and variation in rates of murder, nonnegligent manslaughter, rape, burglary, robbery, and aggravated assault in both countries.

150. Connor, Walter D. (1973). "Criminal Homicide, U.S.S.R./U.S.A.: Reflections on Soviet Data in a Comparative Framework," *Journal of Criminal Law and Criminology*, 64(1): 111-117. Annotations.

Compares Soviet and U.S. criminal homicide data. Examines Soviet and U.S. homicide data derived from previous studies, sex distribution, victim/offender relationship, motive, location and method of homicide, and the influence of alcohol. Discusses findings which include variations in the patterns of homicide in both cultures.

151. Cornell, Claire Pedrick and Richard J. Gelles (1982). "International Perspectives on Spouse Abuse," *Focus on Women*, 3: 171-184. Bibliography.

Questions the claim that U.S. families are more violent than those in other societies. Reviews spouse abuse literature in England, Canada, West Germany, Scotland, Greece, Cyprus, Sicily, Portugal, Japan, India, and Africa. Compares spouse abuse definitions. Discusses common approaches and models used in spouse abuse research.

152. Court, J. H. (1976). "Pornography and Sex-Crimes: A Reevaluation in the Light of Recent Trends Around the World," *International Journal of Criminology and Penology*, 5: 129-157. Bibliography.

Argues that research findings denying a causal relationship between pornography and sex-crimes are premature and inconclusive. Critically reviews various cross-cultural data to support this claim. Outlines common myths about pornographic literature. Discusses legal policy changes in the U.S., Sweden, Denmark, Britain, Amsterdam, and Australia. Provides sex-crime rates for the U.S., Copenhagen, Australia, New Zealand, England and Wales, London, South Australia, and Singapore.

153. Daly, Martin and Margo Wilson (1988). *Homicide*. New York: Aldine De Gruyter. Bibliography, xii + 328pp.

Proposes a causal theory of criminal behavior that reflects Darwinian natural selection. Focuses on the psychology of individual characteristics which are determined through a complex evolutionary process of the mind, and suggests that various types of violence, especially homicide, stem from this process. Discusses infanticide, parricide, gender, and marital homicide. Chapter 12 analyses cross-national variation in homicide rates.

154. Eekelaar, John M. and Sanford N. Katz (eds.) (1978). *Family Violence: An International and Interdisciplinary Study*. Toronto: Butterworths. Appendices, notes, vii + 572pp.

Thirty-five essays that examine various psychological and sociological dynamics of family violence. Themes include rape, wife battering, child and interspousal abuse, and methodological, theoretical and legal aspects in England, the U.S., Belgium, Canada, India, Arabia, France, Amsterdam, Denmark, Australia, and South Africa.

155. Egger, Steven A. (1990). *Serial Murder: An Elusive Phemonenon*. New York: Praeger. Notes, bibliographies, xii + 235pp.

Eleven essays that deal with numerous aspects of serial murder, serial murderers, and serial murder victims. Most of the essays depend on U.S. data, although Chapter 5 (by Richard H. Doney) is on England. Chapters 10-11, written by the editor, address issues of future research.

156. Feierabend, Ivo K., Rosalind L. Feierabend and Betty A. Nesvold (1969). "Social Change and Political Violence: Cross-National Patterns." Pp.632-687 in Hugh Davis Graham and Ted Robert Gurr (eds.), *The History of Violence in America: Historical and Comparative Perspectives*. New York: Praeger. Appendix, bibliography.

Investigates the empirical relationships among social and industrial change and political violence in 84 nations from 1948 to 1965. Examines political development and stability, and modernization, and measures socioeconomic changes.

157. Feirabend, I.K. and R.L. Feirabend (1966). "Aggressive Behaviors within Politics, 1948-1962: A Cross-National Study," *Journal of Conflict Resolution*, 10: 249-271. Bibliography.

Uses three theoretical propositions to compare aspects of political aggression in numerous countries. Tests for (1) levels of frustration and conflict, (2) relationship between modernity and political stability, and (3) prediction of political instability over time. Provides estimation rates for many countries, including Australia, Britain, Belgium, Ireland, Thailand, Colombia, Cuba, Hungary, Paraguay, Iceland, the U.S.S.R., and the U.S.

158. Ferracuti, Franco, Renato Lazzari, and Marvin E. Wolfgang (1970). "A Study of the Subculture of Violence Thesis." Pp.87-146 in Franco Ferracuti, Renato Lazzari, and Marvin E. Wolfgang (eds.), *Violence in Sardinia*. Rome: Mario Bulzoni. Appendices.

Investigates the utility of Wolfgang and Ferracuti's subculture of violence thesis as a cultural explanation of high violent crime rates. Compares violent and non-violent officially sanctioned criminal groups from Sardinia and other parts of Italy. Methodology and data classification provided.

159. Fiala, Robert and Gary LaFree (1988). "Cross-National Determinants of Child Homicide," *American Sociological Review*, 53: 432-445. Notes, bibliography, appendices.

Examines the causes of child homicide in 18 countries. Derives hypothesis from theories of social organization, social structure, culture of violence, and social isolation. Data include World Health Organization child homicide rates, World Bank unemployment rates, professional status of women (ILO), and female students (UNESCO). Findings suggest a correlation between economic stress associated with female labor participation, social barriers, and child homicide.

160. Fingerhut, Lois A. and Joel C. Kleinman (1990). "International and Interstate Comparisons of Homicide Among Young Males," *Journal of the American Medical Association*, 263(24): 3292-3295. Annotations.

Compares homicide rates in the U.S., Scotland, New Zealand, Israel, Norway, Finland, Canada, Australia, Sweden, Belgium, The Netherlands, Switzerland, France, Greece, Ireland, Poland, England and Wales, Portugal, Denmark, West Germany, Japan, and Austria. Examines the statistical contribution of young males to U.S. rate, and offers interstate comparisons.

161. Gartner, Rosemary (1990). "The Victims of Homicide: A Temporal and Cross-National Comparison," *American Sociological Review*, 55(1): 92-106. Bibliography.

Introduces a paradigm for the purpose of examining cross-cultural variations in homicide rates for 18 modern democratic countries during 1950-1980. The model proposed controls for social, theoretical and cultural factors and their relationship to homicide and victimization levels. Reviews relevant theoretical literature.

162. Gastil, Raymond D. (1971). "Homicide and a Regional Culture of Violence," *American Sociological Review*, 36(3): 412-427. Notes, bibliography.

Tests Wolfgang and Ferracuti's [see # 218] thesis about the subculture of violence in the context of the high homicide rates in the U.S. compared with those of most other countries. Finds that the persistent Southern cultural tradition of violence explains much of the regional variations in U.S. homicide rates far better than factors such as income, education, degree of urbanization, and age.

163. Geis, Gilbert and Robley Geis (1979). "Rape in Stockholm: Is Permissiveness Relevant?" *Criminology*, 17(3): 311-322. Notes, bibliography.

Investigates the relationship between cultural permissiveness and forcible rape. Compares officially reported rape statistics for Stockholm, Sweden, with the U.S. cities of Hartford, Duluth, Harrisburg, and Long Beach during 1970-1977. Discusses methodological limitations and probable differences in the cross-cultural interpretation of sexual attitudes. Reviews relevant criminological literature.

164. Gelles, Richard J. (1987). "What to Learn from Cross-Cultural and Historical Research on Child Abuse and Neglect: An Overview." Pp.15-30 in Richard J. Gelles and Jane B. Lancaster (eds.), *Child Abuse and Neglect: Biosocial Dimensions*. New York: Aldine De Gruyter. Bibliography.

Comprehensive examination of the advantages and methodological limitations of historical and comparative research on child abuse and neglect. Outlines contemporary myths of child abuse. Identifies methodological obstacles which hinder comparative and historical child abuse research, including definitional problems, lack of official and historical data, and diversity in cultural values and meanings. Reviews some comparative child abuse findings.

165. Gelles, Richard J. and Claire Pedrick Cornell (1983). "International Perspectives on Child Abuse," *Child Abuse and Neglect*, 7: 375-386. Bibliography.

Surveys international child abuse and neglect literature in Sweden, the U.S., Canada, India, Britain, Australia, Italy, France, Poland, and Yugolslavia. Addresses cross-national legal and cultural variations in definitions of abuse and control techniques. Reviews psychological, social, and economic factors reportedly associated with child abuse in developed and developing cultures.

166. Gelles, Richard and Ake W. Edfeldt (1986). "Violence Towards Children in the United States and Sweden," *Child Abuse and Neglect*, 10: 501-510. Bibliography.

Describes inconclusive findings of a study that used national interview data to compare violence towards children in the U.S. and Sweden. Examines variations in laws, types of victimization, and socio-cultural factors related to incidence. Outlines methodology.

167. Gelles, Richard J. and Jane B. Lancaster (eds.) (1987). *Child Abuse and Neglect: Biosocial Dimensions*. New York: Aldine De Gruyter. Bibliographies, xii + 334pp.

This collection of 13 interdisciplinary essays offers a biosocial perspective on child maltreatment. Essays examine historical, evolutionary, ecological, comparative and cross-cultural aspects of child abuse, child neglect, and parental investment theory. Countries examined include Japan, England, Sweden, China, Poland, the U.S.S.R., Australia, New Zealand, and the U.S. Some attention given to developing countries. Reviews relevant child abuse literature.

168. Graham, Hugh Davis and Ted Robert Gurr (eds.) (1969). *The History of Violence in America: Historical and Comparative Perspectives*. New York: Praeger. Notes, bibliographies, appendices, xxxvi + 822pp.

Contains 22 historical and comparative essays on the patterns and degree of violence in the U.S. and various European countries. Themes include historical factors, processes of violence, repression, and cross-cultural comparison of social conflict and violence. Addresses collective violence in European societies, comparative studies on civil strife and fragment cultures, war, domestic turmoil, and cross-cultural patterns of social change and political violence. Appendix 2 discusses selection procedures for comparison.

169. Gurr, Ted Robert (1968). "A Causal Model of Civil Strife: A Comparative Analysis Using New Indices," *American Political Science Review*, 62(4): 1104-1124. Annotations.

Reports findings of a comparative analysis which utilizes data from 114 polities to examine several types of civil strife. Investigates the relationship between the degree of civil strife and relative deprivation theory. Outlines methodology. Findings support relative deprivation theory.

170. Gurr, Ted Robert (1969). "A Comparative Study of Civil Strife." Pp.572-632 in Hugh Davis Graham and Ted Robert Gurr (eds.), *The History of Violence in America: Historical and Comparative Perspectives*. New York: Praeger. Bibliography, appendicees.

Reviews findings of studies about civil strife in 110 countries and colonies during 1961-1965. Compares, interprets, and assesses various aspects of civil strife, including violence and protest. Includes methodological discussion.

171. Gurr, Ted Robert (1976). *Rogues, Rebels and Reformers: A Political History of Urban Crime and Conflict*. Beverly Hills, California: Sage. Annotations, xii + 192pp.

A comparative historical study of the politics of crime and conflict in London, Stockholm, Sydney, and Calcutta from 1800 to date. Examines the relationship between crime and conflict and policies and institutions. Chapter 1 of Part II examines crime trends for theft, murder and assault, and white-collar offenses.

172. Gurr, Ted Robert (1981). "Historical Trends in Violent Crime: A Critical Review of the Evidence," *Crime and Justice:*

An Annual Review of Research (Michael Tonry and Norval Morris eds., Chicago, Illinois: University of Chicago Press), 3: 295-353. Bibliography.

Historical and comparative analysis of violent crime trends and their relationship to cultural and social changes in Western societies. Includes analysis of the U.S., England and Wales, and the Scandinavian countries from the thirteenth century onwards. Focuses on murder and assault. Reviews official and historical crime data, methodological difficulties, correlative features, and impressions. Briefly discusses nineteenth- and twentieth-century crime trends in Germany, France, Switzerland, Japan, and Austria.

173. Gurr, Ted Robert (1989). "Historical Trends in Violent Crime: Europe and the United States." Pp. 21-54 in vol.1 of Ted Robert Gurr (ed.), *Violence in America: The History of Crime*. 2 vols. Newbury Park, California: Sage. Annotations.

Shows that the increase of violent crime during and after the 1960s in Europe and the U.S. has followed a much longer downward trend. Supports this argument with analyses of violent crime rates in medieval, early modern, and contemporary England, and of nineteenth- and twentieth-century rates in the U.S. Compares violent crime trends in Europe and Australia.

174. Gurr, Ted Robert, Peter N. Grabosky, and Richard C. Hula (1977). *The Politics of Crime and Conflict: A Comparative History of Four Cities*. Beverly Hills, California: Sage. Annotations, xii + 792pp.

An historical and cross-cultural examination of the politics of crime, urban conflict, and public order in London (1800-1970s), Stockholm (1750-1970s), Sydney (1788-1970s), and Calcutta (1800-1970s). Investigates historical and contemporary institutional processes and emergent public control mechanisms. Discusses methodology.

175. Haft-Picker, Cheryl (1980). "Beyond The Subculture of Violence: An Evolutionary and Historical Approach to Social Control." Pp.181-210 in Graeme R. Newman (ed.), *Crime and Deviance: A Comparative Perspective*. Beverly Hills, California: Sage. Bibliography.

Introduces a framework for the comparative study of violence that respects cultural variation. Defines feuding as an evolutionary form of violence in the cultural development of formal social control systems. Numerous illustrations refer to Middle East, Hungary, Arabia, Yugoslavia, and Albania. Discusses the limitations of subculture of violence theory.

176. Hansmann, Henry B. and John M. Quigley (1982). "Population Heterogeneity and the Sociogenesis of Homicide", *Social Forces*, 61(1): 206-224. Notes, bibliography.

Tests the claim that social heterogeneity is conducive to high homicide rates. Uses cross-sectional data from a sample of 58 nations. Finds that population heterogeneity in ethnicity, language, religion, and income is a significiant causal factor in homicide.

177. Hartz, Louis (1969). "A Comparative Study of Fragment Cultures." Pp.107-127 in Hugh Davis Graham and Ted Robert Gurr (eds.), *Violence in America: Historical and Comparative Perspectives*. New York: Praeger. Bibliography.

Follows the history of collective violence in cultural settlements in the U.S. and various parts of Europe, including England, Ireland, Sweden, France, Spain, and Germany. Discusses the historical links among the impact of the migratory process (characterized by cultural fragmentation), interfragment competition, and collective organization. Provides historical examples of collective violence in Europe and suggests an analogy with the U.S.

178. Hauge, Ragnar and Preben Wolf (1974). "Criminal Violence in Three Scandinavian Countries," *Scandinavian Studies in Criminology*, 5: 25-33. Bibliography.

Utilizes survey data to compare criminal victimization in Denmark, Norway, and Finland from 1971 to 1972. Identifies variation in officially reported and in victimization survey data, degree of violence, demographic factors, time and place of violent act, and victim compensation. Finds Denmark and Norway have lower rates than Finland, although few of the violent acts reported are serious.

179. Hoffer, Peter C. and N.E.H. Hull (1981). *Murdering Mothers: Infanticide in England and New England 1558-1803*. New York: New York University Press. Annotations, appendices, xxii + 211pp.

Investigates the ascendancy of contemporary infanticide law in England and New England during 1558-1803. Employs historical data to examine the causes of infanticide and changes in infanticide laws and prosecutions. Discusses the relationships among cultural, socio-economic and environmental factors, the occurrence of infanticide, and judicial and legal changes.

180. Homero, J. and E. Yearwood (1974). "Firearms and Interpersonal Relationships in Homicide: Some Cross-National Comparisons." Pp.114-127 in Marc Riedel and Terence P. Thornberry (eds.), *Crime and Delinquency: Dimensions of Deviance*. New York: Praeger. Notes, bibliography.

Examines cross-cultural variation in firearm availability, firearm use, and interpersonal relationships for both victims and offenders. Data drawn from U.S., Brazil, India, Mexico, England, and Denmark. Findings suggest a strong correlation between criminal homicide and primary social relationships, although the links between firearm availability and homicide remain inconclusive.

181. Hughes, Graham (1964). "The Crime of Incest," *Journal of Criminal Law, Criminology and Police Science*, 55(3):322-331. Annotations.

An historical outline and comparison of incest laws in the U.S. and England. Discusses incest etiology, influenced by the writings of Freud. Refers to few exceptional cases where universal incest taboo is absent, namely, among royal family members in ancient Egypt, in Inca Peru, and in Hawaii. Describes incest acts, familial relations, concealment, and traumatic consequences.

182. Jenkins, Philip and Fred Hutchings (1983). "New Patterns of Urban Riots: Miami and Liverpool." Pp.69-85 in Israel L. Barak-Glantz and Elmer H. Johnson (eds.), *Comparative Criminology*. Beverly Hills, California: Sage. Bibliography.

Compares patterns of urban riots in Miami (U.S.) in 1980 and Liverpool (England) in 1981. Refers to previous riots in England and the U.S., discusses similar/dissimilar features of the 1980/ 1981 riots, and identifies the relationship between political and economic factors and the riots in both countries. Recommendations refer especially to non-confrontational police tactics.

183. Jerath, Bal K., Paul E. Larson, and Jesse F. Lewis (1982). *Homicide: A Bibliography of Over 4,500 Items*. Augusta, Georgia: Pine Tree Publications. xvi + 600pp.

A comprehensive bibliography of homicide. Entries relevant to various aspects of homicide include interdisciplinary, historical, and theoretical items; statistical data (pp.400-452 concern 'other countries of the world'); victimization; methods, causes, and investigation of murder; case studies; legal considerations; and prevention and control.

184. Johansson, S. R. (1987). "Neglect, Abuse, and Avoidable Death: Parental Investment and the Mortality of Infants and Children in the European Tradition." Pp.57-93 in Richard J. Gelles and Jane B. Lancaster (eds.), *Child Abuse and Neglect: Biosocial Dimensions*. New York: Aldine De Gruyter. Bibliography.

Uses historical child and infant mortality data to investigate parenting patterns and avoidable child deaths in pre-industrial Europe. Examines changes in preindustrial ideological and religious beliefs, reproductive practices, parental investment in children's lives, and economic factors. Provides infant mortality data for Sweden and England.

185. Korbin, Jill E. (1987). "Child Maltreatment in Cross-Cultural Perspective: Vulnerable Children and Circumstances." Pp.31-55 in Richard J. Gelles and Jane B. Lancaster (eds.), *Child Abuse and Neglect: Biosocial Dimensions*. New York: Aldine De Gruyter. Bibliography.

Uses cross-cultural literature to analyze contingent situations which place children at risk and which may exacerbate child abuse and neglect. Discusses methodological impediments to cross-cultural analysis of child abuse. Offers suggestions that would enhance cross-cultural research, such as the investigation of circumstances that cultivate or prevent child abuse and neglect.

186. Krahn, Harvey, Timothy F. Hartnagel and John W. Gartrell (1986). "Income Inequality and Homicide Rates: Cross-National Data and Criminological Theories," *Criminology*, 24(2): 269-295. Notes, bibliography, appendix.

Employs relative deprivation theory, information derived from previous studies, and Interpol data for the years 1960, 1965, 1971 and 1975. Finds a positive correlation between income inequality and rates of criminal homicide. Findings support relative deprivation theory, especially in democratic political systems. Reviews alternative theories. Provides income and homicide rates for many countries.

187. Laurence, Michael D., John R. Snortum, and Franklin E. Zimring (eds.) (1988). *Social Control of the Drinking Driver.* Chicago: University of Chicago Press. Notes, bibliography, xix + 452pp.

Contains 14 essays on the social control of drinking drivers from the disciplines of biology, criminology, economics, law, psychology, public policy, and sociology. Essays address issues of deterrence and enforcement in traditional and innovative sanctions. Countries examined include Sweden, Finland, Denmark, Norway, Britain, Canada, Federal Republic of Germany, The Netherlands, and the U.S. Several essays are explicitly comparative.

188. Levinson, David (1989). *Family Violence in Cross-Cultural Perspective.* Newbury Park, California: Sage. Appendix, 146pp.

An anthropological study that analyzes the universal form and frequency of family violence. Collects ethnographic literature on 90 preliterate and peasant societies obtained through the Human Relations Area Files. Methodological design includes cross-cultural case studies, clinical comparisons, and sample surveys. Discusses test results, comparative explanations, and preventive directives.

189. Lichtenstein, Michael J. (1984). "An Empirical Test of the Subculture of Violence and Miller's Theory of Lower Class Delinquency," *International Journal of Comparative and Applied Criminal Justice*, 8(2): 139-149. Bibliography.

Utilizes National Crime Survey severity of crime questionnaire data to analyze the empirical consistency of Wolfgang's and Ferracuti's subculture of violence thesis [see # 218] and Miller's theory of lower-class delinquency. Outlines methodological design and reviews relevant subcultural literature. Findings support subculture hypothesis.

190. Lunden, Walter A. (1976). "Violent Crimes in Japan in War and Peace, 1933-74," *International Journal of Criminology and Penology*, 4(4): 349-363. Notes, bibliography.

Utilizes official and research data to examine violent crime trends in Japan during the prewar era of World War II, post-war period (1946-53), and subsequent years. Examines aggregate crime rates, murder, robbery, and rape offenses, and surveys postwar crime patterns.

191. Mahmood, Tahir (1978). "Child Abuse in Arabia, India and the West - Comparative Legal Aspects." Pp. 281-289 in John M. Eekelaar and Sanford N. Katz (eds.), *Family Violence: An International and Interdisciplinary Study.* Toronto: Butterworths. Annotations.

Investigates various aspects of child abuse and assesses the legal responses to it with a parallel comparison in India/Arabia and England/U.S. Discusses obsolete notions of parental authority, the scope and possible causes of child abuse, and the relationships among the nuclear family system, cultural norms, social stress, and increased incidence of child abuse. Outlines the need for legal reform.

192. Maidment, Susan (1978). "The Law's Response to Marital Violence: A Comparison Between England and the U.S.A." Pp.110-140 in John M. Eekelaar and Sanford N. Katz (eds.), *Family*

Violence: An International and Interdisciplinary Study. Toronto: Butterworths. Annotations.

Compares the legal provisions of marital violence and their operation in England and the U.S. Explores the availability, sufficiency, and provision of legal resources. Outlines criminal and civil proceedings in England and Wales and the U.S. and exemplifies legal concepts and responses to marital violence through court cases.

193. McClintock, F.H., and Per-Olof H. Wihström (1990). "Violent Crime in Scotland and Sweden," *British Journal of Criminology*, 30(2): 207-228. Notes, bibliography,

Reports findings from the first part of a larger research project comparing criminal violence in Scotland and Sweden. Discusses problems of comparability and compares the rate, structure, and trends of known violent crime in both countries. Violent crimes of homicide, robbery, and rapes are shown to have registered marked increases in both countries, although Sweden's increase may only reflect better recording practices and and higher rates of reporting.

194. Messner, Steven F. (1982). "Societal Development, Social Inequality, and Homicide: A Cross-National Test of a Durkheimian Model," *Social Forces*, 61(1): 225-240. Notes, bibliography.

Tests Durkheim's thesis in *The Division of Labor* that social development is accompanied by a movement toward greater social inequality and, with the rise of organic solidarity, no overall increase in homicide rates. Thesis is tested for 50 nations with U.N. social data and Interpol homicide data. Finds partial support for thesis.

195. Messner, Steven F. (1980). "Income Inequality and Murder Rates: Some Cross-National Findings," *Comparative Social Research* (ed. Richard F. Tomasson, Greenwich, Connecticut: JAI Press), 3: 185-198. Notes, bibliography, appendix.

Examines the relationship between income inequality and murder rates. Utilizes data on income distribution, GDP per capita, population, population density, and urbanization. Reviews findings of extant cross-national studies. Tentatively concludes the relationship is positive and moderately strong, and is to be explained in terms of Merton's 'social structure and anomie.' Includes data for 39 countries in the 1950s and 1960s.

196. Middendorff, Wolf (1977). "Bank robbers and their victims: historical and criminological perspectives," *Annales internationales de criminologie*, 16(1-2): 179-191. Annotations.

Offers a cross-cultural typology of bank robbers and their victims. Types include the historical bank robber, the modern conventional bank robber, the political robber, and the female robber. Includes a brief typology of victims. Illustrations drawn largely from the U.S. and West Germany.

197. Newman, Graeme (1981). "Causes and Prevention of Violence: A Cross-Country Survey," *International Review of Criminal Policy*, 37: 96-103. Bibliography.

Reviews the findings of a questionnaire sent to United Nations criminal justice and crime prevention correspondents. Outlines the official responses to increased crime rates for robbery, serious and minor assault, violence related to drug abuse, alcohol and drug trafficking, automobile deaths and injuries, public transportation injuries, school violence, extortion, suicide, and violence with guns. Identifies crimes which have reportedly decreased or stabilized. Reports responses about the aetiology of violence and prevention strategies during 1967-1977.

198. O'Malley, Pat (1980). "The Suppression of Social Banditry: Train Robbers in the U.S. Border States and Bushrangers in Australia, 1865-1905," *Crime and Social Justice*, 16: 32-39. Notes, bibliography.

Analyzes how far the decline of social banditry as a form of primitive rebellion is related to the technological development of state control. Outlines organization of social banditry, and examines the fate of train robbers of the Kansas-Missouri region during 1865 to 1905, and their contemporaries the Australian bushrangers, in the face of technological change and police intervention.

199. Otterbein, Keith F. and Charlotte Swanson Otterbein (1965). "An Eye for an Eye, A Tooth for a Tooth: A Cross-Cultural Study of Feuding," *American Anthropologist* 67(6): 1470-1482. Notes, bibliography.

Describes a comparative study of feuding in 50 societies. Data drawn from the Human Relations Area Files. Tests three hypotheses derived from functional, evolutionary, and intersocietal relations approaches. Examines the relationship between feuding and socio-structural and political variables. Findings suggest a link between low level political integration and increased internal social conflict.

200. Porkorny, Alex D. (1965). "A Comparison of Homicide in Two Cities," *Journal of Criminal Law, Criminology and Police Science*, 56(4): 479-487. Annotations.

Attempts to replicate parts of Wolfgang's study of homicide [see # 216]. Compares the findings of Wolfgang's criminal homicide analysis of Philadelphia during 1948-1952 with data derived from the Houston Police Department files during 1958-1961. Briefly compares the Houston data with a previous 1945-1949 Houston homicide study. Examines victim/offender relationship, including interpersonal association, race and sex.

201. Porkorny, Alex D. (1965). "Human Violence: A Comparison of Homicide, Aggravated Assault, Suicide and Attempted Suicide," *Journal of Criminal Law, Criminology and Police Science*, 56(4): 488-497. Annotations.

Utilizes case file data derived from the Houston Police Department to examine homicide, aggravated assault, suicide, and attempted suicide patterns in Houston, Texas, from 1955 to 1962. Examines site and time of occurrence; census track residence for those victims and offenders involved in violence, and distribution rates for age, days of the week, sex, race, and ethnic group. Compares findings among categories studied.

202. Quinney, Richard (1965). "Suicide, Homicide and Economic Development," *Social Forces*, 43(3): 401-406. Annotations.

Uses World Health Organization homicide, suicide, and age-specific data for 1953-1960 to compare suicide and homicide rates in 48 countries. Findings suggest influence of economic development on suicide and homicide, and that the two latter are separate phenomena.

203. Reite, Martin, and John P. Capitanio (1987). "Child Abuse: A Comparative and Psychobiological Perspective." Pp.149-174 in Richard J. Gelles and Jane B. Lancaster (eds.), *Child Abuse and Neglect: Biosocial Dimensions*. New York: Aldine De Gruyter. Bibliography.

Explores cross-cultural, ecological, environmental, and biological aspects of human and nonhuman primates to determine which contribute to child abuse, neglect, and physiological disturbance. Discusses early separation and attachment, experimental data, observations, and theoretical implications.

204. Rockett, Ian R.H., and Gordon Smith (1989). "Homicide, Suicide, Motor Vehicle Crash, and Fall Mortality: United States' Experience in Comparative Perspective," *American Journal of Public Health*, 79(10): 1396-1400. Annotations.

Uses World Health Organization data for 1980 to compare mortality rates from motor vehicle crashes, falls, suicide, and homicide in the U.S., France, Japan, West Germany, and the U.K. Mortality rates are shown to vary dramatically by country, age, and sex.

205. Ross, H. Laurence (1982). *Deterring the Drinking Driver*. Lexington, Massachusetts: D.C. Heath. Notes, bibliography, xxvii + 129pp.

A widely-acclaimed study of the complex conditions under which legal sanctions can be applied to control drinking drivers. Discusses the methodological and conceptual problems of measuring the deterrent effects of OUI legislation. Examines and compares laws and law enforcement in Sweden, Finland, Norway, the U.K., France, The Netherlands, Canada, New Zealand, Australia, and the U.S.

206. Sanday, Peggy Reeves (1981). "The Socio-Cultural Context of Rape: A Cross-Cultural Study," *Journal of Social Issues*, 37(4): 5-27. Bibliography.

Examines the frequency, meaning, and 'function' of rape using extensive secondary literature on tribal societies. Argues that rape in tribal societies is part of a cultural configuration that includes interpersonal violence, male dominance, and sexual separation. Discusses common types of rape in several tribal cultures and characterizes rape-prone societies as those in which male dominance is prominent.

207. Schwartz, Martin D. (1988). "Ain't Got No Class: Universal Risk Theories of Battering," *Contemporary Crises*, 12(4):373-392. Notes, bibliography.

Criticizes classless risk theories of physical violence which ignore socio-economic considerations. Argues for a comprehensive theoretical analysis of battering syndrome and risk. Reviews relevant feminist analyses, theories, and methodologies. Advances several theoretical propositions which correlate class with gender relationships.

208. Scrimshaw, Susan C.M. (1984). "Infanticide in Human Populations: Societal and Individual Concerns." Pp.439-462 in Glenn Hausfater and Sarah Blaffer Hardy (eds.), *Infanticide: Comparative and Evolutionary Perspectives*. New York: Aldine. Bibliography.

Employs data from 1976 study to compare the frequency of infanticide in 112 preindustrial cultures. Discusses variation in definitions, types of, and motives for infanticide among the early Japanese and Chinese, the Machigenga, the Andean Indians, the Kamchadal of Siberia, the Yaudapu Enga of New Guinea, Eskimo groups, and the Yanomamo of Venezuela. Discusses problems of accuracy in mortality data.

209. Sloan, John Henry, Arthur L. Kellerman, Donald T. Reay, *et al.* (1988). "Handgun Regulations, crime, assaults, and homicide: a Tale of Two Cities," *New England Journal of Medicine*, 319(19): 1256-1262. Bibliography.

Compares rates of assault and homicide in Seattle (Washington) and Vancouver (Canada) from 1980 to 1986. Finds that Seattle has significantly higher age- and sex-adjusted homicide rates than Vancouver, even though overall crime rates of both cities are similar. Higher Seattle rates attributed to greater use of handguns. Recommends restricting handgun access.

210. Sloan, John Henry, Frederick P. Rivara, Donald T. Reay, James A. J. Ferris, and Arthur L. Kellerman (1990). "Firearm Regulations and Rates of Suicide: A Comparison of Two Metropolitan Areas," *New England Journal of Medicine*, 322(6): 369-373. Bibliography.

Examines the relationship between acts of suicide and firearm regulations during 1985-1987 in Washington and British Columbia. Measures socio-economic characteristics, suicide rates, risk estimates, and official gun ownership registration rates. Findings suggest a possible relationship between firearm regulations and homicide, but not suicide. Recognizes the unreliability of official suicide statistics.

211. Tilly, Charles (1989). "Collective Violence in European Perspective." Pp.62-100 in Ted Robert Gurr (ed.), *Violence in America: Protest, Rebellion, Reform*. Newbury Park, California: Sage. Notes, bibliography.

Sketches the complex social processes lying behind the actual occurrence of collective violence in western countries in the last 200 years. Main conclusion is that collective violence is endemic to the Western political process, and major changes in it derive from major changes in political systems. Countries referred to include Britain, France, Italy, Belgium, Prussia, The Netherlands, and Germany. Makes several comparisons with the U.S.

212. Tutorow, Norman E. (ed.) (1986). *War Crimes, War Criminals, and War Crimes Trials.* Westport, Connecticut: Greenwood Press. Appendices, glossary, xx + 548pp.

Comprehensive annotated bibliography of war crimes, war criminals, and war crimes trials. Contains chapters on references; general works and subsidiary topics; early war crimes, war criminals, and trials from ancient times to World War I; a variety of World War II war crimes and war criminals, including the holocaust; and war crimes and trials in Asia and Vietnam.

213. Viano, Emilio C. (ed.) (1989). *Crime and Its Victims: International Research and Public Policy Issues.* New York: Hemisphere Publishing. Notes, bibliographies, xiii + 317pp.

Contains 27 papers from the Fourth International Institute on Victimology held in Tuscany, Italy in August 1987. Themes include victimization dynamics and interaction, the victim and the justice system, the child victim, sexual victimization, and public policy. Largely single-culture studies from the U.S., Portugal, Italy, Canada, India, West Germany, Australia, Israel, the U.K., The Netherlands, France, and Turkey. Policy recommendations provided.

214. Wasikhongo, Joab M. (1976). "Uniformities in Aggravated Assaults in St. Louis (Missouri) and Mombasa (Kenya): A Cross-Cultural Replication," *International Journal of Criminology and Penology*, 4(1): 9-24. Notes, bibliography.

Examines aggravated assault patterns and their contributing factors in Mombasa, Kenya during 1971. Compares findings with a 1961 study of St. Louis, Missouri. Outlines methodological design, which tests the relationship between situational interaction and violent behavior. Findings outline similarities and differences in both studies.

215. West, Donald (1983). "Sex Offenses and Offending," *Crime and Justice: An Annual Review of Research* (Michael Tonry and Norval Morris eds., Chicago, Illinois: University of Chicago Press), 5: 183-233. Bibliography.

Compares historical and contemporary sex offense trends and policy changes. Categorizes patterns of recorded sexual offenses in Denmark, the U.S., England and Wales, Canada, West Germany, and Yugoslavia. Discusses the relationship between offender characteristics and other forms of crime, causal theories, and treatment and victimological research, including the demedicalization of some forms of deviant sexual behavior. Reviews various relevant research studies and judicial procedures.

216. Wolfgang, Marvin E. (1958). *Patterns in Criminal Homicide.* London: Oxford University Press. Bibliography, notes, appendices, xiv + 413pp.

Investigates criminal homicide in Philadelphia, Pennsylvania, from 1948 to 1952. Focuses on the victim and offender in the homicide drama, the victim-offender relationship, and the offender after the crime. Includes analysis of age, race, and gender. Chapter 3 compares various homicide/race data in the U.S., Austria, Germany, Italy, Ceylon, and China.

217. Wolfgang, Marvin E. (1981). "Surveying Violence Across Nations: A Review of the Literature with Research and Policy Recommendations," *International Review of Criminal Policy*, 37: 62-95. Bibliography.

A comprehensive survey of selected types of international violent crimes, both authorized and unauthorized. Countries include Australia, Sri Lanka, Kenya, Japan, Turkey, India, Belgium, Finland, Portugal, Switzerland, Mexico, Ireland, Scotland, Spain, the U.S., New Zealand, France, Greece, and Peru. 'Unauthorized crimes include homicide, aggravated assault, and robbery; 'authorized' crimes include torture, genocide, vigilantism, riots, labor strikes, and terrorism. Discusses previous literature, crime definitons, and explanations. Drafts research and policy recommendations.

218. Wolfgang, Marvin E. and Franco Ferracuti (1967). *Subculture of Violence: Towards an Integrated Theory in Criminology.* London: Tavistock. Notes, bibliography, xxiii + 387pp.

Offers a systematic theory ('the subculture of violence') for understanding the effects of values favorable to violence. Uses an interdisciplinary approach to study subcultures, aggression, and violent crimes, especially homicide. Reviews findings, cross-cultural homicide case studies, social control, treatment, and preventive directives. Provides official homicide rates for a number of years in a variety of societies, and offers numerous cross-cultural comparisons.

5

Crimes Against Property

219. Abbott, Daniel J. (1980). "Liberation Movements and Robbery: A Comparative Analysis of Uganda and the United States," *International Journal of Comparative and Applied Criminal Justice*, 4(2): 165-178. Bibliography.

Compares the causes of rising robbery rates in Uganda and the U.S. during the 1960s. Reviews various theories of political changes in both countries. Provides official crime rates for robbery and murder/manslaughter in the U.S during 1960-1975, and robbery rates in Uganda for the years 1955, 1959, 1964 and 1968. Findings suggest the influence in both countries of social forces on increased robbery rates.

220. Bacon, Margaret K., Irvin L. Child, and Herbert Barry III (1981). "A Cross-Cultural Study of Correlates of Crime." Pp.174-188 in Louise I. Shelley (ed.), *Readings in Comparative Criminology*. Carbondale, Illinois: Southern Illinois University Press. Annotations.

Examines crime correlations in a sample of 48 preliterate societies, selected on the basis of geographical diversity and adequate data on aboriginal child-training practices. Focuses on the psychological and sociological determinants of crime. Findings outline general crime correlations, especially those relating to theft and personal crime.

221. Balvig, Flemming (1988). *The Snow-White Image: The Hidden Reality of Crime in Switzerland.* Translated by Karen Leander. New York: Oxford University Press. Notes, bibliography, 123pp.

An important examination of Switzerland's crime patterns, demonstrating their firm links with structural forces and social control agencies. Earlier studies of Swiss crime [e.g., see # 306] are shown to have numerous methodological and conceptual problems. Undermines the image of Switzerland as a crime-free society and exposes the fact that Switzerland has much higher crime rates (e.g., economic crimes and money laundering) than is usually believed, because police deflate official records and because strict social controls are exerted on potential deviants.

222. Clinard, Marshall and Daniel J. Abbott (1976). "Community Organization and Property Crime: A Comparative Study of Social Control in the Slums of an African City." Pp.186-206 in James F. Short, Jr. (ed.), *Delinquency, Crime and Society*. Chicago, Illinois: University of Chicago Press. Notes, bibliography.

Uses official and unoffical crime data to compare crime and residents' perception in two urban slum communities in Uganda. Discusses demographic and cultural features. Attributes different theft rates to different social organization of both communities. Outlines methodology and research findings.

223. Danziger, Sheldon (1976). "Explaining Urban Crime Rates," *Criminology*, 14(2): 291-296. Notes, bibliography.

Uses an economic model of urban crime to examine the relationships among unemployment, population density, and crime rates for robbery and burglary. Outlines methodological design and reports empirical findings. Supports a positive correlation among economic factors, population density, and crime rates.

224. Stack, Steven (1982). "Social Structure and Swedish Crime Rates: A Time-Series Analysis, 1950-1979," *Criminology*, 20(3-4): 499-513. Bibliography.

Uses Interpol time-series data for the years 1950-1979 to test an opportunity theory of crime in Sweden. Briefly reviews methodological and theoretical difficulties of cross-cultural analysis and relevant criminological literature. Finds that the percentage increase in Swedish property crime, despite Swedish income redistribution, exceeded that of the U.S. in this period.

6

Economic and Political Crime

225. Box, Steven (1983). *Power, Crime, and Mystification*. London: Tavistock. Bibliography, xi + 257pp.

Challenges the view that most serious crime is committed by the relatively powerless. Uses material from Britain, the U.S., Canada, and Holland to argue that most serious crime is committed by persons and organizations in positions of power. Numerous cross-cultural generalizations on corporate crime, police crime, and on gender and crime.

226. Cebulak, Wojciech (1989). "White-Collar and Economic Crime: An International Perspective," *International Journal of Comparative and Applied Criminal Justice*, 13(1): 31-40. Notes, bibliography.

Proposes a theory of international white-collar crime. Identifies similarities between national and international types of white-collar and economic crimes. Discusses international efforts to curb white-collar and economic crime, including those of the United Nations and the Council of Europe. Reviews the 1979 U.N. adoption of the Draft International Agreement on Illicit Payments and the U.N. Code on Restrictive Business Practices.

227. Clarke, Michael (1980). "Syndicated Crime in Britain?", *Contemporary Crises*, 4(4): 403-420. Notes, bibliography.

Identifies the complexities of syndicated crime and the potential bases for its existence in Britain. Includes a theoretical discussion of syndicated crime and a review of the literature. Argues that drugs and commercial sex are two potential areas for syndicated crime. Compares British aspects with other countries, including the U.S., Denmark, China, Turkey, Iran, Vietnam, and Laos.

228. Council of Europe (1977). "Criminological Aspects of Economic Crime. Strasbourg: Council of Europe", *Collected Studies in Criminological Research*, vol.15. Notes, bibliographies, 180pp.

Three reports presented in 1976 to the Twelfth Conference of Directors of Criminological Research Institutes. First report discusses forms of economic crime in the Federal Republic of Germany, Belgium, France, England, and Switzerland. Second report examines sociological and psychological aspects of economic crime, and advances a general typology. Third report discusses anticrime policies, including international differences in law, judicial systems, and punishment.

229. Heidenheimer, Arnold J. (ed.) (1970). *Political Corruption: Readings in Comparative Analysis*. New York: Holt, Rinehart and Winston. Bibliographies, ix + 582pp.

A collection of 58 essays on the characteristics of political crime. Part 1 covers interdisciplinary, institutional and behavioral aspects of political corruption. Part 2 provides an administrative and comparative analysis of political corruption. Part 3 deals with state crime in the U.S., England, France, Germany, and in various developing countries such as the Philippines, Kenya, India, New Guinea, and Pakistan. Part 4 examines modernization and corruption.

230. Holland, Robert C. (1984). "Problems in the Investigation of White Collar Crime: A Case Study," *International Journal of Comparative and Applied Criminal Justice*, 8(1): 21-41. Bibliography.

Provides an illustrative case study to demonstrate the rampant legal and research difficulties of investigating and litigating white-collar crimes. Focus is the ability of criminal offenders to use their social status to their advantage, particularly in business crimes.

231. Ingraham, B.L. and Kazuhiko Tokoro (1969). "Political Crime in the United States and Japan: A Comparative Study," *Issues in Criminology*, 4(2): 145-170. Annotations, appendix.

A comparison of conceptual and procedural differences in the legal processes of political crime in Japan and the U.S. Describes the doctrine of political crime, legal concepts, and offender treatment for various political crimes such as treason. Appendix, annotations.

232. Ingraham, Barton L. (1979). *Political Crime in Europe: A Comparative Study of France, Germany and England*. Berkeley, California: University of California Press. Bibliography, appendices, xiii + 380pp.

A comparative historical analysis of the characteristics of political crime and control mechanisms and their links with other forms of criminality from 1789 to 1970. Case studies include France, Germany, and Britain. Discusses the nature of political crime and definitional problems.

233. Jenkins, Philip and Gary W. Potter (1986). Organized crime in London: A comparative perspective," *Corruption and Reform*, 1(3): 165-187. Bibliography.

Attempts to describe, despite a paucity of available data, the nature and structure of organized crime in London, its organization, ethnic composition, and activities. Explores 'money movers,' official corruption, gambling, drugs, and labor racketeering. Identifies significant differences in activities and scale of organized crime in Britain and the U.S.

234. Los, Maria (1980). "Economic Crimes from a Comparative Perspective." Pp.251-293 in Graeme R. Newman (ed.), *Crime and Deviance: A Comparative Perspective*. Beverly Hills, California: Sage. Notes, bibliography.

Contains a fourfold classification of economic crimes. Examines and compares the relationship between a variety of economic crimes and the economic system in developed capitalist and communist countries. Outlines economic offenses such as petty theft, crimes on the black market, and crimes by corporate enterprises.

235. Los, Maria (1982). "Crime and Economy in the Communist Countries." Pp.121-137 in Peter Wickman and Timothy Dailey (eds.), *White-Collar Crimes: Multidisciplinary and Cross-National Perspectives*. Lexington, Massachusetts: Lexington Books and D.C. Heath. Bibliography.

Discusses the relationship between national communist economies and crime. Focuses on the problems and inherent contradictions in communist economies, their organizational and political imperatives, and processes of production. Discusses various economic crimes such as bribery, theft of nationalized property, state crimes, and the production of black market enterprise. Refers to the U.S.S.R., Poland, and other eastern European countries.

236. Los, Maria (1983). "Economic Crimes in Communist Countries." Pp.39-57 in Israel L. Barak-Glantz and Elmer H. Johnson (eds.), *Comparative Criminology*. Beverly Hills, California: Sage. Bibliography.

Discusses types of economic crimes which threaten communist processes of production and distribution of goods in the U.S.S.R. and Poland. Outlines common economic crimes, such as report padding, black market activities, and legal penalties. Describes the relationship between economic crimes and the organizational forces of communist economies.

237. Los, Maria (1987). "The Double Economic Structure of Communist Societies," *Contemporary Crises*, 11(1): 25-58. Bibliography.

Explores and compares the scope and mechanics of subcultural ('second') economies and their relationship to formalized economic systems in the U.S.S.R., Poland, and Hungary. Includes a description of extant second economies, parallel legal and economic characteristics, and the extent of crime.

238. Los, Maria (ed.) (1990). *The Second Economy in Marxist States*. New York: St. Martin's Press. Notes, bibliographies, 240pp.

A series of comparative essays on the second economy in the U.S.S.R., Poland, Hungary, Romania, Yugoslavia, Cuba, Nicaragua, China, Angola, and

Tanzania. Essays outline (official) state economy and (unofficial) second economy and their relationship to the national economy. Discusses historical, organizational, and legal aspects of second economies and their consequences.

239. Lupsha, Peter (1981). "Drug Trafficking: Mexico and Colombia in Comparative Perspective," *Journal of International Affairs*, 35(1): 95-115. Annotations.

Compares drug trafficking and control policies in Mexico and Colombia and their effects on both countries and on the U.S. Reviews relationship between drug production and economic and political conditions. Provides U.S. financial aid rates, 1973-1980; drug trafficking income estimates, 1975-1979; and income distribution rates derived from marijuana sales in 1978.

240. Mack, J.A. and H.J. Kerner (1976). "Professional and Organized Crime - A Comparative Approach," *International Journal of Criminology and Penology*, 4(2): 113-128. Bibliography.

Discusses the differences between professional crime and organized ('syndicated') crime in Europe and the U.S. and estimates the volume of these crimes in both regions. Reviews relevant comparative literature on the organizational aspects of professional and organized crime. Discusses the relationship between the study of criminal organization and deviancy theory.

241. Martens, Frederick T. and Frank Pulley (1984). "Cross-Cultural Reflections of Organized Crime," *International Journal of Comparative and Applied Criminal Justice*, 8(1): 63-74. Bibliography.

Discusses the intrinsic relationships among cultural ideology, perception, and organized crime in Britain and the U.S. Outlines structural, political, and conceptual differences between British and U.S. organized crime activities. Describes the unique association between history and organized crime in the U.S.

242. Nepote, Jean (1974). "Interpol and Organized Crime," *International Criminal Police Review*, 282: 230-236.

From a symposium on organized crime held at the Bundeskriminalamt in 1974. Outlines three types of organized crime, including premeditated, professional, and syndicated crime. Characterizes and explicates a cross-cultural concept of organized crime. Suggests preventive organized crime measures on a national and international level.

243. Reasons, Charles E. and Colin H. Goff (1980). "Corporate Crime: A Cross-National Analysis." Pp.126-141 in Gilbert Geis and Ezra Stotland (eds.), *White-Collar Crime: Theory and Research*. Beverly Hills, California: Sage. Bibliography.

Historically examines cross-national legislative origins of free enterprise and economic competition in Canada, the U.S., Australia and the U.K. Investigates the relationship between specific laws and their literal and symbolic interpretation of corporate crime.

244. Reuter, Peter (1984). "Social Control in Illegal Markets." Pp.29-58 in vol. 2 of Donald Black (ed.), *Toward a General Theory of Social Control.* 2 vols. Orlando, Florida: Academic Press. Notes, bibliography.

Examines the mechanisms and rules of social control developed by participants in large-scale organized markets of illegal goods and services. Examines conceptual issues in dispute settlement and arbitration. Presents a series of six stylized accounts of dispute settlement in New York City area, involving stolen liquor, bookmakers, jewelry theft, stock manipulation, and informants.

245. Sheleff, Leon (1982). "International White-Collar Crime." Pp.39-57 in Peter Wickman and Timothy Dailey (eds.), *White-Collar and Economic Crime: Multidisciplinary and Cross-National Perspectives.* Lexington, Massachusetts: Lexington Books and D.C. Heath. Annotations.

Discusses the relationship between international corporate crime and international law. Reviews relevant legal and sociological literature and challenges corporate irresponsibility and legitimation of international white-collar crime, including pollution, and the looting of cultural/archaeological artifacts. Argues for international legal cooperation in the prosecution of international white-collar offenses.

246. Simon, David R. and D. Stanley Eitzen (1986). *Elite Deviance.* Boston: Allyn and Bacon. Annotation, x + 290pp.

Analyses the structural causes of political and corporate elite deviance in the U.S. and its enduring and systematic links to capitalist economy. Addresses definitional problems. Occasional references to other cultures, such as Panama. Describes the nature and conceptualization of elite deviance, economic and political corruption, environmental consequences, and international dimensions.

247. Tanzi, Vito (1982). *The Underground Economy in the United States and Abroad.* Lexington, Massachusetts: D.C. Heath. Notes, bibliography, appendix, x + 340pp.

Nineteen essays by economists on the definition, nature, and extent of underground or 'second' economies in the U.S., the U.K., Italy, Norway, Sweden, U.S.S.R., Canada, Colombia, Australia, and Israel. Cross-cultural generalizations provided.

248. Tiedemann, Klaus (1977). "Phenomenology of Economic Crime." Pp.9-68 in 'Collected Studies in Criminological Research', vol.xv,*Criminological Aspects of Economic Crime.* Strasbourg: Council of Europe. Bibliography.

Report presented to the Twelfth Conference of Directors of Criminological Research Institute in 1976. Outlines comparative similarities in forms of economic crime, such as cartel offenses, computer crimes, and insurance fraud. Examines sanctions and crime prevention in the Federal Republic of Germany, Belgium, France, England, and Switzerland. Discusses legal, political, and economic aspects of economic crime.

249. Turk, Austin T. (1982). *Political Criminality: The Defiance and Defense of Authority.* Beverly Hills, California: Sage Publications. Bibliography, 232pp.

An analysis of the processes of crime and political organization. Examines the relationship between political criminality and political policing. Discusses the transformative process of power into authority (e.g., policing) and the essence of legal order, characterized as ideal types, in various countries including Britain, Canada, and the U.S.

250. Wickman, Peter and Timothy Dailey (1982). *White-Collar and Economic Crime: Multidisciplinary and Cross-National Perspectives*. Lexington, Massachusetts: Lexington Books. Bibliographies, xviii + 285pp.

Fourteen essays presented at a symposium held at S.U.N.Y, Potsdam in February 1980. Most of the essays raise important issues about the relations between white-collar/economic crime and social organization in general, but only a few contain an explicit empirical focus outside the U.S. These latter include crime and economy in communist countries (Maria Los) and the safety of British offshore oil installations (W.G. Carson).

251. Wilson, Paul R., Gilbert Geis, Henry N. Pontell, Paul Jesilow, and Duncan Chappell (1985). "Medical Fraud and Abuse: Australia, Canada, and the United States," *International Journal of Comparative and Applied Criminal Justice*, 9(2): 25-34. Bibliography.

Compares medical fraud and abuse related to health care benefit insurance programs in Australia, Canada, and the U.S. Focuses on variations in types of medical abuse and fraud, occupational and economic factors, and medical and legal responses.

7

Transnational Corporate Crime

252. Baker, James C. (1985). "The International Infant Formula Controversy: A Dilemma in Corporate Social Responsibility," *Journal of Business Ethics*, 4: 181-190. Annotations.

Examines the international distribution of breast-food substitutes. Analyzes corporate and non-corporate reactions to this controversy and strategic marketing changes. Addresses legal, social and health aspects, research findings, with special reference to Third World nations such as India.

253. Braithwaite, John (1979). "Transnational Corporations and Corruption: Towards Some International Solutions," *International Journal of the Sociology of Law*, 7(2): 125-142. Notes,bibliography.

Outlines various strategic maneuvers, such as bribery, corruption and rule bending, which are used by transnational corporations to evade international laws and regulations. Discusses the problems of controling corporate illegalities through the greater use of law, and suggests that a simple solution is more vigorous prosecution with less complex and formal laws.

254. Esbjörnsson, Esbjörn (1974). "International Criminality in Sweden," *Scandinavian Studies in Criminology*, 5: 11-23.

Describes how expanded communication and transportation networks have contributed to increased international crime (e.g., export/import of drugs, spirits, pornography, stolen cars, etc.) in Sweden during the last decade. Outlines the characteristics and evolution of current aspects of international crime, such as the availability of increased drug and pornographic markets.

255. Fein, Helen (1978). "A Formula for Genocide: Comparison of the Turkish Genocide (1915) and the German Holocaust (1939-1945)," *Comparative Studies in Sociology: An Annual Compilation of Research* (ed. Richard F. Tomasson, Greenwich, Connecticut: JAI Press), 1: 271-294. Notes, bibliography.

A political description of the murders of Armenian and Jewish groups. Traces the political history, ideology, and motives behind genocide. Discusses the influence of war and postwar behavior, ethnic discrimination against Jews, 'gypsies' and Armenians, and genocide in Turkey and Germany to achieve political ends.

256. Michalowski, Raymond and Ronald C. Kramer (1987). "The Space Between Laws: The Problem of Corporate Crime in a Transnational Context," *Social Problems*, 34(1): 34-53. Notes, bibliography.

Critically discusses transnational concepts of corporate crime. Outlines United Nations efforts to codify transnational corporate crime, and the role of U.S. business interests in thwarting their scope and application, especially in Third World countries where lenient laws facilitate corporate crime in areas such as working conditions, environmental pollution, and consumer safety. Argues that international legal codes should regulate corporate violations and other socially injurious acts.

8

Correlates of Crime: Age, Class, Gender and Race

257. Aday, Ron H. (ed.) (1988). *Crime and the Elderly: an Annotated Bibliography.* Westport, Connecticut: Greenwood Press. xiii +118pp.

Annotated bibliography of crime and the elderly. Contains two major parts ('crimes against the elderly' and 'the elderly as criminals') and a part on resources and information.

258. Adler, Freda (1977). "The Interaction Between Women's Emancipation and Female Criminality: A Cross-Cultural Perspective," *International Journal of Criminology and Penology*, 5(2): 101-112. Anotations, bibliography.

Examines the relationship between contemporary gender equality (social and economic) and increased female crime rates. Compares crime data for various countries from 1937 to 1972, including the U.S., the Federal Republic of Germany, Japan, Australia, Canada, England and Wales, New Zealand, Brazil, Poland, and India. Discusses increasing female crime trends in robbery, murder, larceny, arson, homicide, and extortion.

259. Adler, Freda (1981). "International Concern in Light of the American Experience." Pp.1-13 in Freda Adler (ed.), *The Incidence of Female Criminality in the Contemporary World.* New York: New York University Press. Annotations.

Examines international changes in female crime trends. Addresses increased female crime rates in developed and developing nations, international academic interest, and theoretical and judicial interpretations. Compares male/female regional crime distribution rates from 1970 to 1975 for the Middle East, North Africa, Eastern Europe, Latin America, the Caribbean, Western Europe, Oceania, and North America.

260. Adler, Freda (1981). *The Incidence of Female Criminality in the Contemporary World.* New York: New York University Press. Annex, bibliography, viii + 275pp.

A collection of 13 single-culture studies of changes in female crime trends. Countries include the U.S., The Netherlands, Finland, Norway, England and Wales, Germany, Poland, Hungary, Nigeria, Egypt, Argentina, Venezuela, India, and Japan. Topics include rising female crime rates and their cultural interpretation, judicial responses, and the alleged relationship between female crime and the feminist movement.

261. Boles, Jacqueline and Charlotte Tatro (1978). "Legal and Extra-Legal Methods of Controlling Female Prostitution: A Cross-Cultural Comparison," *International Journal of Comparative and Applied Criminal Justice*, 2(1): 71-85. Bibliography.

Examines and compares formal and informal mechanisms for reducing and controlling female prostitution in a variety of cultures. Includes legal, regulatory and political discussion, social and communal features, and decriminalization strategies.

262. Bowker, Lee H. (1985). "The Effects of National Development on the Position of Married Women in the Third World: The Case of Wife-Beating," *International Journal of Comparative and Applied Criminal Justice*, 9(1): 1-13. Bibliography.

Examines the relationship between modernization and wife-beating in Third World countries. Compares findings with studies conducted in industrialized nations. Reviews contemporary research and discusses the relationship between socioeconomic status and wife-beating and child abuse. Includes victimization rates for sex crimes (1973-1980) and rapes (1977-1980) in Australia, Denmark, England and Wales, Federal Republic of Germany, France, Japan, New Zealand, Norway, Sweden, the U.S., Brunei, India, Indonesia, Korea, Kuwait, Lesoto, Malaysia, Malawi, Sri Lanka, and Turkey.

263. Brown, Julia (1952). "A Comparative Study of Deviations from Sexual Mores," *American Sociological Review*, 17(2): 135-146. Annotations.

A classic anthropological study that examines 110 societies in the Human Relations Area Files to establish the putative existence of universal sexual taboos. Correlates frequency of deviant offenses with degree of punitive severity. Finds that adultery, rape, and incest are most often tabooed and most severely punished. Features methodological description, ethnographic, typological and punitive hierarchies, correlational data, findings and impressions.

264. Brunsten, M., J. Graham, N. Herriger, and P. Malinowski (eds.) (1986). *Youth Crime, Social Control and Prevention: Theoretical Perspectives and Policy Implications. Studies from Nine Diffferent Countries.* Wuppertal: International Document and Study Centre for Conflicts of Youth, Bergische University. Bibliographies, 236pp.

A collection of 19 essays on various aspects of youth crime. Essays discuss theoretical and conceptual issues related to deinstitutionalization, cross-cultural variations in juvenile justice, policy implications, and general processes of criminalization. Regions include North America, Japan, Nigeria, Israel, The Netherlands, Britain, West Germany, and Latin America.

265. Caplan, Aaron and Marc LeBlanc (1985). "A Cross-Cultural Verification of a Social Control Theory," *International Journal of Comparative and Applied Criminal Justice*, 9(2): 123-138. Notes, bibliography.

A comparative test of Hirschi's social control theory of delinquency in Montreal, Canada. Provides a detailed review of Hirschi's methodological analysis. Supports partial confirmation. Discusses the similarities and differences in both study findings, and attributes differences to variations in the nature of the respective samples.

266. Cavan, Ruth Shonle and Jordan T. Cavan (1968). *Delinquency and Crime: Cross-Cultural Perspectives*. Philadelphia, Pennsylvania: J.B. Lippincott. Bibliography, 244pp.

Single-culture analyses of crime and delinquency in 14 societies. Countries include Mexico, India, the U.S.S.R., England, The Netherlands, Germany, Italy, Denmark, and Norway. Addresses cultural variation in concepts of crime, legal factors, and rural and urban crime trends in urban, rural, primitive, tribal, and folk societies. Examines the relationships among war, urban and industrial development, and crime definitions and meanings.

267. Chang, Dae (1987). "Violence Against Women in the Family: A National and International Perspective," *International Journal of Comparative and Applied Criminal Justice*, 11(2): 153-157.

Reviews issues discussed at an international conference on family violence held in 1986 at Vienna, Austria. Focuses on family violence as a serious international problem; its definition; the consequences of family violence for women, men, children and society; the causes of family violence; the roles of social institutions and the criminal justice system as preventive agents; and the need for crisis intervention. Proposes remedies for cultural equality and incident reduction.

268. David, Pedro R. and Joseph W. Scott (1973). "A Cross-Cultural Comparison of Juvenile Offenders, Offenses, Due Processes and Societies: The Cases of Toledo, Ohio and Rosario, Argentina," *Criminology*, 11(2): 183-205. Bibliography.

Utilizes juvenile court data for the years 1966 and 1967, observation findings, and published reports to examine juvenile delinquency patterns, due process of law, social customs and socio-economic variations in Toledo, Ohio and Rosario, Argentina. Discusses dominant juvenile crime patterns of both countries.

269. DeFleur, Lois B. (1967). "Delinquent Gangs in Cross-Cultural Perspective: The Case of Cordoba," *Journal of Research in Crime and Delinquency*, 4(1): 132-141. Annotations.

Compares delinquent gang patterns in Cordoba, Argentina, with the U.S. Utilizes judicial and interview data to describe Cordoba gang subcultures and compares crime and social characteristics with U.S. delinquent subculture theories. Outlines differences found in U.S. and Cordoba gang subcultures.

270. DeFleur, Lois B. (1967). "Ecological Variables in the Cross-Cultural Study of Delinquency," *Social Forces*, 45(4): 556-570. Annotations.

Addresses the need for ecological studies when applying U.S. delinquency theories abroad. Tests the applicability of U.S. subculture theory in Cordoba, Argentina. Sample consists of juvenile court data for 1958-1961. Examines spatial distribution and theoretical implications and compares patterns with U.S. Findings suggest ample variance between these two countries, indicating a need for critical application of U.S. theories to other cultures.

271. DeFleur, Lois B. (1969). "Alternative Strategies for the Development of Delinquency Theories Applicable to Other Cultures," *Social Problems*, 17(1): 30-39. Bibliography.

Re-examines A.K. Cohen's delinquency theory in an attempt to demonstrate the inaccuracies of applying U.S. delinquency theories to other cultures. Addresses relevant comparative concerns, such as diverse cultural meaning of delinquency. Stresses the need for critical theoretical and cultural evaluation. Offers alternative research strategies.

272. DeVos, George (1980). "Delinquency and Minority Status: A Psychocultural Perspective." Pp.130-180 in Graeme R. Newman (ed.), *Crime and Deviance: A Comparative Perspective*. Beverly Hills, California: Sage. Notes, bibliography.

Adopts an anthropological and psychocultural approach to study delinquency patterns cross-culturally. Uses family court records for Japanese cities to examine the relationships among socio-economic status, urban migration, psychological variables, family dynamics, and delinquency. Compares findings with previous delinquency studies conducted in other countries.

273. Eve, Raymond and Ursula Cassani (1984). "The Etiology of Juvenile Delinquency: The United States and Switzerland Compared," *International Journal of Comparative and Applied Criminal Justice*, 8(2): 163-174. Notes, bibliography.

Compares juvenile delinquency in the U.S. and Switzerland. Emphasizes methodological difficulties. Focus includes juvenile crime trends and cultural features. Critically reviews previous Swiss crime analyzes, particulary Clinard's [see # 306]. Offers theoretical and pragmatic comparative hypotheses for future research.

274. Ferracuti, Franco and Simon Dinitz (1974). "Cross-Cultural Aspects of Delinquent and Criminal Behavior." Pp.18-34 in Marc Riedel and Terence P. Thornberry (eds.), *Crime and Delinquency: Dimensions of Deviance*. New York: Praeger.

Discusses key problems in comparative criminology, including the lack of reliable data, legal differences; methodology, and cultural variation in the processing of offenders. Urges multidisciplinary approach in comparative criminology. Reviews findings from a 1966-1969 interdisciplinary study that identified and compared psychological, physiological, and social characteristics of delinquent and non-delinquent juvenile groups in Puerto Rico. Methodological design and difficulties discussed.

275. French, Laurence (1977). "A Cultural Perspective Toward Juvenile Delinquency," *International Journal of Comparative and Applied Criminal Justice*, 1(2): 111-121. Bibliography.

Investigates the influence of cultural factors on juvenile delinquency. Compares the etiology of juvenile delinquency in the U.S. with traditional folk cultures in the Nuer, the Hopi, the Keraki Indians of New Guinea, and the Arunta of Central Australia. Discusses cultural group allocation, subcultural determinants, social control features, socialization practices, and the relationship between anomie and deviance.

276. Friday, Paul C. (1974). "Research on Youth Crime in Sweden: Some Problems in Methodology," *Scandinavian Studies*, 46(1): 20-30. Bibliography.

Tests the applicability of the theories of differential opportunity and differential association in Sweden. Uses sample of crimes committed from 1966 to 1967. Discusses difficulties of comparative research. Findings suggest the importance of interpersonal associations. Reviews comparative variation in youth crime in Sweden and U.S.

277. Friday, Paul C. (1980). "International Review of Youth Crime and Delinquency." Pp.100-129 in Graeme R. Newman (ed.), *Crime and Deviance: A Comparative Perspective*. Beverly Hills, California: Sage. Bibliography.

Utilizes cross-cultural studies to identify structural, institutional, social, and familial conditions which contribute to youth crime. Discusses delinquency rates and trends, role and status of youth, and links between social institutions and delinquency. Outlines implications for comparative analysis.

278. Friday, Paul C. and Jerald Hage (1976). "Youth Crime in Postindustrialized Societies: An Integrated Perspective," *Criminology*, 14(3): 347-368. Bibliography.

Offers a theoretical framework which combines relevant juvenile delinquency theories with the Durkheimian concept of social integration. Attempts to establish a connection between macro- and micro-deviance analysis. Discusses the importance of the interaction of forces among community, familial network, peer and role relationships, structural adaptation, socialization, and youth crime.

279. Friday, Paul C. and V. Lorne Stewart (eds.) (1977). *Youth Crime and Juvenile Justice: International Perspectives*. New York: Praeger. Bibliographies, xii + 181pp.

A collection of 14 essays on various aspects of juvenile crime and justice in the industrialized societies of the U.S., England, Scotland, Belgium, Israel, and Puerto Rico. Topics include delinquency analysis, juvenile justice systems, and social policies for crime prevention and offender rehabilitation.

280. Hartjen, Clayton A. and S. Priyadarsini (1984). *Delinquency in India: A Comparative Analysis*. New Brunswick, New Jersey: Rutgers University Press. Bibliography, appendices, xiv + 252pp.

Examines juvenile delinquency and societal reaction in India. Investigates various aspects of delinquency, including types of delinquency, occurrence and distribution of delinquency, delinquency legislation, social control processes, and treatment of delinquency. Comparatively reviews urban/rural delinquent and nondelinquent features. Describes and compares official arrest statistics in India and the U.S. for 1974. Appendices outline methodology.

281. Hollander, Paul (1969). "A Converging Social Problem: Juvenile Delinquency in the U.S.S.R and the U.S.," *British Journal of Criminology*, 9(2): 148-166. Bibliography.

Discusses social problems, especially juvenile delinquency, in the U.S.S.R. and the U.S. Focuses on structural dissimilarities and comparable and incomparable aspects of delinquency in both countries. Suggests that a positive relationship exists between boredom and deviance in both countries, while alcohol and delinquency are more closely related in the U.S.S.R. than in the U.S. Outlines the influence of industrialization on delinquency.

282. Jasinski, Jerzy (1966). "Juvenile Delinquency in Poland 1961-1967 (Extent, Structure, Adjudicated Means)," *Archiwum Kryminologii*, 4: 229-240. Annotations.

Explores alternative methods for identifying different aspects, scope, and adjudication of juvenile crime in Poland. Study uses official data from 1961 to 1967 to examine male/female conviction rates for juvenile delinquency. Compares adjudicated guilt rates and corrective measures with previously assembled years.

283. Jencks, Christopher (1987). "Genes and Crime," *New York Review of Books*, February 12: 33-41

A short review of Wilson and Herrnstein's *Crime and Human Nature* and Currie's *Confronting Crime*. Examines the strengths and weaknesses of arguments supporting the influence of genes on criminal behavior. Uses comparative homicide data to show that social and cultural variables are more important determinants of crime than genes.

284. Malewska, Hanna and Vincent Peyre (1976). "Juvenile Delinquency and Development: A Cross-National Study," *Sage Research Papers in the Social Sciences*, no. 90-031, vol. 4. Notes, appendices, 40pp.

A research paper presented in 1972 at the Budapest Round Table Conference on Theory and Practice in Cross-National Survey Research. Describes some findings of a cross-national project on juvenile delinquency and economic development. Countries examined include France, Hungary, Poland, and Yugoslavia. Appendices provide a published list of project documents, project institutes and researchers, and other papers given at the Conference.

285. Martin, Robert G. Jr., and Rand D. Conger (1980). "A Comparison of Delinquency Trends: Japan and the United States," *Criminology*, 18(1): 53-61. Bibliography.

Compares official court and police data in order to evaluate and contrast juvenile crime trends in the 1970s in Japan and the U.S. Outlines methodological design which includes demographic and legal data for both countries. Offers comparative delinquency rates and findings.

286. McClellan, Dorothy Spektorov (1987). "Soviet Youth: A View from the Inside," *Crime and Social Justice*, 29: 1-25. Bibliography.

Interdisciplinary study that investigates juvenile delinquency as a social problem in the U.S.S.R. Includes a brief historical overview of delinquency in the U.S.S.R. Explores Soviet socialist philosopy; socialization patterns; familial, institutional, and judicial processes; type and range of delinquency and prevention methods.

287. Meadow, Arnold, Stephen I. Abramowitz, Arnold de la Cruz, and German Otalora Bay (1981). "Self-Concept, Negative Family Affect, And Delinquency," *Criminology*, 19(3): 434-448. Bibliography.

Offers a test of control theory outside the standard Anglo-Saxon terrain. Investigates the relationships among self-concept, the influence of family dynamics, and juvenile delinquency for various social classes in Mexico. Methodology includes controls for comparing class status, delinquent self-concept, and judicial intervention.

288. Miller, Eleanor (1983). "International Trends in the Study of Female Criminality: An Essay Review," *Contemporary Crises*, 7(1): 59-70. Annotations.

A critical review of three books on female criminality. Argues that many contemporary studies of female criminality seriously err in attributing the alledged post-1960s rise in female crime rates to three factors: the contemporary women's liberation movement, subjective shifts in sex role attitudes and orientations, and increased female participation in the labor force.

289. Rosenquist, Carl M, and Edwin I. Megaree (1969). *Delinquency in Three Cultures*. Austin, Texas: University of Texas Press. Bibliography, appendices, language glossary, xvi + 554pp.

Uses cross-cultural method and juvenile court samples to compare social, psychological, and medical differences between delinquent and nondelinquent groups in lower-class Anglo-American, Mexican, and Mexican-American cultures. Briefly reviews delinquency research and theories. Detailed methodological description and discussion provided.

290. Shaskolsy, Eliezer, Ruth Erez, and Walter C. Reckless (1970). "A Cross-Cultural Comparison of Delinquent and Non-Delinquent Boys." Pp.98-118 in Shlomo Shoham (ed.), *Israel Studies in Criminology*, vol 1. Tel-Aviv: Gometh Publishing House. Bibliography.

Compares studies of delinquent and non-delinquent adolescent males conducted in Israel and the U.S. Examines the relationship between the effect of community structure and decreased delinquency. Uses U.S. psychological instruments (e.g., the Minnesota Multiple Personality Inventory) and tests hypotheses with differential opportunity theory and value orientation theory. Discusses methodology, findings, and theoretical interpretation.

291. Skinner, William F. (1986). "Delinquency, Crime, and Development: A Case Study of Iceland," *Journal of Research in Crime and Delinquency*, 23(3): 268-294. Notes, bibliography.

Investigates the nature of delinquency in Iceland. Collects distributional, correlational, and multivariate data on a variety of illegal acts from an urban sample of adolescents aged 13-16 in Reykjavic. Data tend to support the conclusion that minor and major forms of crime and delinquency are less prevalent than in other modernized countries, partly because of Iceland's egalitarianism and its very low unemployment rate.

292. Toby, Jackson (1981). "Affluence and Adolescent Crime." Pp.18-43 in Louise I. Shelley (ed.), *Readings in Comparative Criminology*. Carbondale, Illinois: Southern Illinois University Press. Annotations.

Investigates the relationships among affluence, parental social control, and adolescent crime. Focuses on rising crime rates in many developed countries, including the U.S., Japan, Sweden, and Canada. Provides juvenile crime rate increases in Japan for selected years from 1941 to 1964. Outlines some supportive cross-cultural case studies.

293. Varma, Paripurnanand (1985). "Cultural and Sociological Aspects of Juvenile Delinquency: An Analysis of Manuel López-Rey's Thesis." Pp.707-716 in Pedro R. David (ed.), *Crime and Criminal Policy*. Pub. 25. Milan: United Nations Social Defence Research Institute. Annotations.

Assesses López-Rey's thesis in *Police and Juvenile Delinquency* about the relationship between cultural attitudes and behavior. Stresses the importance of cultural relativism in comparative analysis. Refers to juvenile crimes committed by males and females, including rape, robbery, murder, and theft. Reviews a variety of cross-cultural studies of delinquency in India, England, Asia, Australia, West Germany, and the U.S.

294. Vaz, Edmund W., and John Casparis (1981). " A Comparative Study of Youth Culture and Delinquency: Upper Middle-Class Canadian and Swiss Boys." Pp.56-77 in Louise I. Shelly (ed.), *Readings in Comparative Criminology*. Carbondale, Illinois: Southern Illinois University Press. Annotations.

Measures self-reported attitudes and social and delinquency data for upper middle-class adolescents in Canada and Switzerland. Outlines measurement findings for peer orientation, attitudes toward fighting, intimacy, sexual behavior, and 14 delinquent activities. Compares similarities and differences found in Canadian and Swiss samples.

295. Viccica, Antoinette D. (1985). "Women, Crime and Criminal Justice: The United Nations Search for Fairness." Pp.729-734 in Pedro R. David (ed.), *Crime and Criminal Policy*. Pub. 25.

Milan: United Nations Social Defence Research Institute. Bibliography.

Discusses the United Nations' recognition of gender-related crime and justice issues. Topics include increased female crime rates reported in a number of developed and developing countries, administrative equality, sanctions, and treatment methods. Refers to international data on drug trafficking and violence.

296. Wagatsuma, Hiroschi, and George A. DeVos (1984). *Heritage of Endurance: Family Patterns and Delinquency Formation in Urban Japan*. Berkeley and Los Angeles: University of California Press. Bibliography, xii + 500pp.

Employs a psychocultural approach to the study of delinquency formation in Japan. Investigates the patterns and social processes of fifty urban Japanese families. Concludes that Japanese tradition and socialization patterns contribute to low rates of delinquency. Suggestions offered for further areas of comparative analysis.

297. Weinberg, Kirson S. (1964). "Juvenile Delinquency in Ghana: A Comparative Analysis of Delinquents and Nondelinquents," *Journal of Criminal Law, Criminology, and Police Science*, 55(4): 471-481. Annotations.

Examines the influence of family, school and peer relations on juvenile delinquency in Ghana, West Africa. Methodology includes male and female delinquent and non-delinquent group samples. Discusses findings in a cross-cultural context.

298. Weinberg, S. Kirson (1976). "Shaw-McKay Theories of Delinquency in Cross-Cultural Context." Pp.167-185 in James F. Short, Jr. (ed.), *Delinquency, Crime and Society*. Chicago, Illinois: University of Chicago Press. Bibliography.

Compares types of delinquency derived from early Shaw and McKay studies with contemporary U.S. and West African crime in three types of urban society. These societies are described as Western laissez-faire, Western welfare-oriented, and Western with tribal features. Discusses ecological and paradigmatic aspects and delinquent subculture thesis. Criticizes some previous delinquent studies.

299. Wilson, Nanci Koser (1983). "An International Perspective on Women and Criminology." Pp.99-118 in Elmer H. Johnson (ed.), *International Handbook of Contemporary Developments in Criminology: General Issues and the Americas*. Westport, Connecticut: Greenwood Press. Notes, bibliography.

A theoretical analysis of changing trends in female crime for numerous crime categories in many nations. Utilizes data taken from various research studies. Discusses the putative relations among emancipation, increased social interaction, and rising female crime rates. Charts international female crime trends.

9

Underdevelopment and Modernization

300. Adler, Freda (1983). *Nations Not Obsessed with Crime.* Littleton, Colorado: Fred B. Rothman. Notes, bibliography, xx + 204pp.

Explores crime prevention strategies and formal and informal social control processes in the low crime rate countries of Switzerland, Ireland, Bulgaria, German Democratic Republic, Costa Rica, Peru, Japan, Nepal, Algeria, and Saudi Arabia. Findings suggest a relationship between social cohesion ('synnomie') and low crime rates. Appendices provide crime/socioeconomic variables.

301. Baldwin, John (1979). "Ecological and Areal Studies in Great Britain and the United States," *Crime and Justice: An Annual Review of Research* (eds. Norval Morris and Michael Tonry, Chicago: University of Chicago Press), 1: 29-66. Notes, bibliography.

Overview of those aspects of the ecological approach to crime that have generated most interest in Britain and the U.S. Includes discussion of University of Chicago research during 1920s and 1930s and the major areal traditions after World War II. Recommends development of Oscar Newman's concept of 'defensible space.'

302. Boerhringer, Gill H. (1977). "Criminology and Neocolonialism: the Case of Papua New Guinea," *Crime and Social Justice*, 8 (Fall/Winter): 58-63. Bibliography.

Essay written while urban crime emerged as a public issue in Papua New Guinea. Argues that recent criminological work on the Third World is a neocolonial prop for increased exploitation of colonized peoples. Examines neo-colonialism in Papua New Guinea and general links between neocolonialism and criminology.

303. Brenner, Harvey M. (1976). "Effects of the Economy on Criminal Behaviour and the Administration of Criminal Justice in the United States, Canada, England and Wales and Scotland." Pp.25-65 in United Nations, *Economic Crises and Crime: Correlations between the State of the Economy, Deviance and the Control of Deviance*. Pub. 15. Rome: United Nations.

Conference summary providing a cross-cultural time-series analysis of the relationship between economic change and crime during 1900-1970. Identifies various theories about the relationships among economic changes, violent crime, and the criminal justice system. Includes methodological interpretation and findings.

304. Clinard, Marshall B. (1960). "A Cross-Cultural Replication of the Relation of Urbanism to Criminal Behavior," *American Sociological Review*, 25(2): 253-257. Annotations.

An analysis of Sweden that replicates an earlier cross-cultural study of the relationship between crime and urbanism. Methodological design consists of selected administration of questionnaire survey and theoretical hypotheses investigating urban rural differences. Reviews methodological difficulties. Findings discussed.

305. Clinard, Marshall B., and Daniel J. Abbott (1973). *Crime in Developing Countries: A Comparative Perspective*. New York: John Wiley. Notes, bibliography, appendices, xv + 319pp.

Examines crime and juvenile delinquency in developing nations. Compares urban/rural crime trends in many developing countries including Uganda, India, Kenya, Mexico, Latin America, Puerto Rico, and Zambia. Investigates the relationship between crime and social change. Discusses a variety of increased crime rates and policy implications in developing countries. Should be read with Balvig [see # 221] and Sumner [see # 351].

306. Clinard, Marshall B. (1978). *Cities with Little Crime: The Case of Switzerland*. Cambridge: Cambridge University Press. Annotations, appendix, xv + 208pp.

A pioneering study of Swiss criminality utilizing a variety of methodological techniques to provide a more precise measure of Swiss crime rates. Findings are compared with other countries, especially Sweden, the U.S., and the Federal German Republic. Should be read with Balvig [see # 221], which seriously challenges Clinard's claim of low Swiss crime rates.

307. Cohen, Stanley (1982). "Western Crime Control Models in the Third World: Benign or Malignant?" *Research in Law, Deviance and Social Control* (ed. Steven Spitzer, Greenwich, Connecticut: JAI Press), 4: 85-119. Notes, bibliography.

Offers a typology of the systematic transfer to Third World countries of three Western crime control models, referred to respectively as 'benign transfer', 'malignant colonialism', and 'paradoxical damage'. Discusses social control ideologies and the historical relationships among imperialism, colonialism, and capitalism and social control systems.

308. Connor, Walter D. (1976). "Deviance, Stress, and Modernization in Eastern Europe." Pp.181-203 in Mark G. Field

(ed.), *Social Consequences of Modernization in Communist Countries.* Baltimore, Maryland: Johns Hopkins University Press. Annotations.

Discusses the relationships among modernization, migration, tension, and trends and types of deviance in the Eastern European countries of Hungary, Poland, Yugoslavia, Czechoslovakia, and Bulgaria. Offers East/West modernization paradigms and some comparative crime data for crimes against persons and property offenses for selected years between 1950 and 1970.

309. David, Pedro R. (1985). "Justice and the Role of the Juridical Institutions Within the Context of Development in Latin America and the Caribbean in Connection with Ecological Problems That Influence the Well-Being of Children and Families." Pp.247-271 in Pedro R. David (ed.), *Crime and Criminal Policy.* Pub. 25. Milan: United Nations Social Defence Research Institute.

Exemplifies Latin American and Caribbean ecological experience to discuss conflicts facing developing nations, juridical institutions, and national and international development. Focuses on the influence of migration, unemployment, industrialization and related social factors on crime, juvenile delinquency, family problems, health and education. Various developing nations examined in Asia, Africa and Central America.

310. Doleschal, Eugene (1981). "Crime and Delinquency Research in Selected European Countries." Pp.217-234 in Louise I. Shelley (ed.), *Readings in Comparative Criminology.* Carbondale, Illinois: Southern Illinois University Press. Annotations.

Outlines selected European crime and post-1963 delinquency literature and compares European and U.S. research types and methods. Countries include Sweden, Germany, The Netherlands, France, Belgium, Denmark, Finland, and Italy. Reviews and assesses European research developments.

311. Ebbe, Obi N. I. (1984). "Ecological Distribution of Juvenile Delinquency in Metropolitan Lagos," *International Journal of Comparative and Applied Criminal Justice*, 8(2): 187-197. Appendix.

Investigates the ecological distribution of juvenile delinquency in metropolitan Lagos and compares findings with those of Western 'environmental' theory. Discusses geographical and methodological features, findings, offense identification, and cultural comparability.

312. Eggleston, Elizabeth (1976). *Fear, Favour or Affection: Aborigines and the Criminal Law in Victoria, South Australia and Western Australia.* Canberra: Australian National University Press. Bibliography, appendices, xix + 397pp.

Compares three Aboriginal cultures and their relationship to the criminal law. Study based on two years fieldwork in Victoria and southern and western Australia. Identifies customary Aboriginal law and institutions and demographic and geographical data. Describes the judicial treatment of Aborigines. Appendices provide various methodological features including offense category, and arrest and prosecution rates for Aborigine and white groups.

313. Encinoza, Argenis Riera, and Rosa del Olmo (1979). "The View from Latin America -- Against Transnational Criminology: A Call for Democratic International Cooperption," *Crime and Social Justice*, 15: 61-67. Annotations.

Two Venezuelan criminologists complain that progressive views on crime and justice are systematically controlled by U.S. criminologists during a U.N. conference. Argues that U.S. penal policies should not be exported to other countries.

314. Ferracuti, Franco (1968). "European Migration and Crime." Pp.189-219 in Marvin E. Wolfgang (ed.), *Crime and Culture: Essays in Honor of Thorsten Sellin*. New York: John Wiley. Annotations.

Examines the relationships between crime and migration, especially migration from Mediterranean to Central and Northern European countries. Reviews different theories and discusses various research findings about types, rates, and trends of crimes by migrants. Suggests migrant crime rate is generally equal to or lower than the rate of host populations.

315. Fish, Mary (1984). "Deterring Sex Sales to International Tourists: A Case Study of Thailand, South Korea, and the Philippines," *International Journal of Comparative and Applied Criminal Justice*, 8(2): 175-186. Bibliography.

Compares sex sales to tourists in the developing societies of Thailand, South Korea, and the Philippines. Identifies how prostitution can be deterred by various social control methods, such as strict legal sanctions for individuals and industries who solicit. Discusses cultural, economic, and legal features, and street and hotel/agency markets.

316. Groves, W. Byron, Richard McCleary, and Graeme Newman (1985). "Religion, Modernization, and World Crime," *Comparative Social Research* (Greenwich, Connecticut: JAI Press), 8: 59-78. Notes, bibliography, appendix,

Attempts to sort out the competing claims of comparative criminologists that modernization can be accompanied by either a decreasing or a rising crime rate. Attributes some discrepancy in the literature to inadequate cross-national crime data and improperly theorized notions of 'modernization.' Finds *inter alia* a positive relation between equality and homicide, and that nations with large school enrollments have low homicide rates.

317. Groves, W. Byron, and Graeme Newman (1986). "Criminal Justice and Development: Some Critical Observations," *International Journal of Comparative and Applied Criminal Justice*, 10(1): 1-16. Notes, bibliography.

Essays examines traditional concepts of development, questioning whether it is as desirable as is commonly made out to be. Suggests that industrial, economic, political, educational, and social forms of development are accomplished at great cost. One such cost is rising crime rates.

318. Groves, W. Byron, Graeme Newman, and Charles Corrado (1987). "Islam, Modernization and Crime: A Test of the Religious

Ecology Thesis," *Journal of Criminal Justice*, 15: 495-503. Bibliography.

Uses data from the United Nations World Crime Survey to examine the relationships among Islamic religion, economic development, and crime rates. Compares 14 Islamic with 33 non-Islamic countries. Islamic countries include Algeria, Bahrain, Cyprus, Egypt, Indonesia, Iran, Iraq, Kuwait, Morocco, Oman, Pakistan, Qatar, Syria, and Turkey. Finds that if economic development is held constant, 'religiosity' does not reduce crime rates significantly.

319. Gurr, Ted Robert (1981). "Contemporary Crime in Historical Perspective: A Comparative Study of London, Stockholm, and Sydney." Pp.103-119 in Louise I. Shelley (ed.), *Readings in Comparative Criminology*. Carbondale, Illinois: Southern Illinois University Press. Annotations.

Compares trends and patterns in official crime data during 1820-1970 in the cities of London, Stockholm, and Sydney. Examines the relationship between the transformation of public order and crime and arrest statistics. Compares arrest and conviction rates for property crimes. Findings and impressions discussed.

320. Herbert, David (1982). *The Geography of Urban Crime*. London: Longman. Bibliography, xii + 120pp.

A contextually designed geographical study of urban crime that draws on theories of spatial and social ecology. Identifies and compares some important regional patterns of crime in urban areas of England, Wales, and the U.S.

321. Horton, John, and Tony Platt (1986). "Crime and Criminal Justice Under Capitalism and Socialism: Towards a Marxist Perspective," *Crime and Social Justice*, 25: 115-135. Bibliography.

Critically assesses trends in comparative criminology in capitalist and socialist societies, emphasizing modernization and radical crime theories. Reviews capitalist and socialist concepts of crime. Discusses why Marxist analysis and World Systems theory offer a viable focus and framework for comparative study of crime in both socialist and capitalist countries.

322. Kick, Edward L., and Gary LaFree. "Development and the Social Context of Murder and Theft, "*Comparative Social Research* (Greenwich, Connecticut: JAI Press), 8: 37-58. Notes, bibliography.

Examines the relationships among social development, family/household density, and theft and murder rates in 40 countries. Relies on Archer and Gartner's Comparative Crime Data File [see Appendix A]. Findings support theories of differential opportunity for theft, and aspects of social inequality and urbanization for murder; also, household density may contribute to both crimes.

323. Krohn, Marvin D. (1976). "Inequality, Unemployment and Crime: A Cross-National Analysis," *Sociological Quarterly*, 17: 303-313. Bibliography.

Utilizes cross-cultural data derived from the World Handbook of Political and Social Indicators (1972), the Yearbook of Labour Statistics (1967), and Interpol data to compare the relationships among economic inequality, unemployment and crime. Examines homicide, property offenses, and absolute crime rates. Methodology and findings discussed. Reviews relevant criminological literature.

324. Krohn, Marvin D. (1978). "A Durkheimian Analysis of International Crime Rates," *Social Forces*, 57(2):654-670. Bibliography, appendix.

Tests Durkheim's theory of the relationship between the division of labor and anomie. Independent variables are taken from the World Handbook of Political and Social Indicators, and include total population figures, degree of urbanization, energy consumption per capita, industrial labor statistics, and satisfaction of social want. Data on homicide and property offenses taken from Interpol. Tentatively concludes that anomie is not related to crime rates with the expected magnitude.

325. Kwasniewski, Jerzy (1984). *Society and Deviance in Communist Poland*. New York: St. Martin's Press. Bibliography, 210pp.

Introduces an interactionist theory of social and judicial repression in Poland. This work creatively seeks to uncover Polish society by unmasking and interpreting culturally accepted concepts of deviance and social control that perpetuate repression. Based in part on national opinion surveys in Poland. Contains comparisons with Brazil, Canada, Italy, Romania, Venezuela, and Yugoslavia.

326. Jankovic, Ivan (1984). "Socialism and the Death Penalty," *Research in Law, Deviance and Social Control* (ed. Steven Spitzer and Andrew T. Scull, Greenwich, Connecticut: JAI Press), 6: 109-137. Notes, bibliography.

Identifies and documents the traditional connections between socialism and the abolition of the death penalty. Discusses the apparent paradox of its retention by its principled opponents. Refers to European Social Democratic programs 1891-1914, the Bolshevik experience, and Eastern Europe.

327. Lombardo, Lucien X. (1984). "Lessons from the Third World for Understanding American Criminal Justice," *International Journal of Comparative and Applied Criminal Justice*, 8(1): 75-83. Bibliography.

Discusses the utility of including Third World historical and contemporary criminal justice literature in U.S. criminal justice academic curricula. Describes Third World ideology and the contexts of criminal justice, such as poverty, urban development, rapid population growth, and political unrest. Outlines invaluable lessons of Third World criminal justice analysis, including increased greater understanding of U.S. criminal justice.

328. Lombardo, Lucien X. (1986). "Nation Building and Social Control: Observations from Ivory Coast and Tanzania," *International Journal of Comparative and Applied Criminal Justice*, 10(1): 41-55. Notes, bibliography.

Employs Eckstein's conceptual model to categorize social polity and political society and compare social control development and nation-building in Ivory Coast and Tanzania. Discusses the political, cultural, and social control changes involved in nation-building, including political and institutional development and methods of dispute resolution.

329. Los, Maria (1988). *Communist Ideology, Law and Crime: A Comparative View of the USSR and Poland.* New York and London: St. Martin's Press. Notes, bibliography, xv + 353pp.

Reviews respective practico-ideological development of the state and criminal justice systems of U.S.S.R. and Poland. Compares class-related common crimes and their relationship to politics and economics. Crimes examined include red-collar; bribery, extortion, and favoritism; economic; pilfering; against communist ethics; and conventional crimes. Focuses on structural and ideological dimensions, contextual features, and variation in crime patterns. Methodological features and findings discussed.

330. Lucas, Stephen A. (1976). "Social Deviance and Crime in Selected Rural Communities of Tanzania," *Cahiers d'Etudes africaines*, 63-64, XVI(3-4): 499-518. Annotations.

Reviews four African rural case studies in order to demonstrate the methodological complications which inhibit accurate analysis of rural crime. Discusses neglected features of rural crime, the importance of defining crime in a relativist fashion and in terms of basic social conflicts and contradictions.

331. Lunden, Walter A. (1963). *War and Delinquency.* Ames, Iowa: Art Press. Bibliography, vi + 88pp.

Examines the relationship between war and increased juvenile delinquency in 13 societies. Compares juvenile crime and changes in conviction rates for prewar, wartime, and postwar World War I and II eras in Germany, England, Russia, France, Ulster, Northern Ireland, Belgium, Holland, Sweden, Norway, Denmark, Japan, Canada, and the U.S. from 1910 to 1958. Discusses age and gender characteristics of delinquency.

332. Mahabir, Cynthia (1985). *Crime and Nation-Building in the Caribbean: the Legacy of Legal Barriers*. Cambridge, Massachusetts: Schenkman Publishing. Notes, bibliography, xiii + 276pp.

Examines the political and legal history of Trinidad and Tobago. Demonstrates a relationship between colonialism's legal and political dominance and the history of crime, legal definitions, and social control in developing third-world nations. Criminalization, or 'Nation-Building', is described as a positive, necessary aspect of social evolution which is utilized in an attempt to challange social injustice.

333. Mesa-Lago, Carmelo (1975). "A Continuum Model for Global Comparison." Pp.92-120 in Carmelo Mesa-Lago and Carl Beck (eds.), *Comparative Socialist Systems: Essays on Politics and Economics*. Pittsburgh, Pennsylvania: University of Pennsylvania Center for International Studies. Annotations.

Outlines a continuum model with social, political, and economic variables. Compares the development of socialism in China, Cuba, U.S.S.R., Czechoslovakia, and Yugoslavia from 1910 to 1970. Outlines methodological problems. Reviews potential uses for the model, such as to examine developmental stages on the basis of economic growth, income distribution, and political stability.

334. Milner, Alan (ed.) (1969). *African Penal Systems.* New York: Frederick A. Praeger. Notes, xiii + 501pp.

Part 1 contains nine essays that describe the penal systems of Ethiopia, Ghana, Kenya, Tanzia, Uganda, Lesotho, Botswana, Swaziland, Liberia, the Congo, The United Arab Republic, and Zambia. Part 2 consists of six essays on various specific issues in African penal processes, including underdevelopment, sentencing, and psychiatry.

335. Mukherjee, Satayansku K. (1981). *Crime Trends in Twentieth-Century Australia.* Sydney, Australia: Australian Institute of Criminology. Notes, bibliography, appendices, xvi + 199pp.

A longitudinal study investigating the relationship between Australia's changing crime patterns and its structural and technological changes from 1900 to 1976. Integrates legal, ideological, and methodological features. Provides some comparative data for England and the U.S.

336. Neuman, W. Lawrence, and Ronald J. Berger (1988). "Competing Perspectives on Cross-National Crime: An Evaluation of Theory and Evidence," *Sociological Quarterly*, 29(2): 281-313. Notes, bibliography.

A comprehensive literature review compares the 'Durkheimian-Modernization,' 'Marxian-World System,' and 'Ecological-Opportunity' perspectives on cross-national crime rates. Finds that empirical evidence provides weak support for propositions derived from each perspective. Recommends that comparative criminology should be integrated with research on economic development and crime in general.

337. Opolot, James S. E. (1980). "Alternatives to Imprisonment in the New States of Africa," *International Review of Criminal Policy*, 36: 19-26. Annotations.

Reviews social control trends and penal policies in Tanzania, Nigeria, Uganda, Kenya, and Somalia. Discusses traditional and contemporary sanctions, the influence of industrialization and urbanization on penal measures, and the dynamic transformation of colonial and post-colonial penal policies.

338. Poklewski-Koziell, Krysztof (1981). "Policies and Programmes with Potential for the Prevention and Control of Violence in the Light of the Experience of Socialist Countries of Eastern Europe," *International Review of Criminal Policy*, 37: 28-37. Bibliography.

Describes historical and legal development of the concept of 'hooliganism' and refers to relevant literature on crime prevention and aetiology. Crimes include homicide, rape, and alcoholism. Countries include Poland, the U.S.S.R., Hungary, Czechoslovakia, and German Democratic Republic.

339. Rizkalla, Samir (1974). "Crime and Criminal Justice in the Developing Countries," *Acta Criminologica*, 7(1): 169-191. Bibliography.

Summarizes discussions presented at the Fifth International Symposium on Comparative Criminology held in Italy in May, 1973. Focuses on corruption, fraud, rape, theft, swindling, murder, counterfeiting, and criminal justice institutions in Latin America, Western Asia, North Africa, and African societies south of the Sahara.

340. Rottman, David B. (1980). *Crime in the Republic of Ireland: Statistical Trends and Their Interpretation*. Dublin, Ireland: Economic and Social Research Institute. Paper No. 102. Bibliography, 158pp.

An excellent investigation of changing official crime statistics, urban/rural crime patterns, and national crime trends in Ireland from 1951 to 1975. Analysis examines the unstated assumption that the experiences of industrial societies like the U.S. and Britain are currently being reenacted in Ireland. Identifies a relationship between increased crime rates and changing social conditions in Ireland.

341. Salas, Luis P. (1980). "The Study of Crime in Marxist Countries: Notes on Methods for Outsiders, with Special Reference to Cuba." Pp.68-99 in Graeme R. Newman (ed.), *Crime and Deviance: A Comparative Perspective*. Beverly Hills, California: Sage. Bibliography.

Examines Cuba as a representative example of a variety of problems confronting comparative criminologists in socialist societies. Discusses the political ideology of Cuban society, the complexity of field investigations, and discrepancies in reporting practices. Suggests various innovative methodological approaches for conducting research in socialist societies.

342. Scandinavian Research Council For Criminology (1974). *Crime and Industrialization (Prestyposti Indystrializatsia)*. Stockholm: Stockholm University Press. Appendix, 284pp.

Fourteen conference papers given at the First Seminar for Criminologists from Socialist and Scandinavian Countries, held in Helsinki in August, 1974. Focus is the cross-cultural relationship between industrialization and crime. Nine essays contribute to this focus; others report on criminological research in Finland, Norway, Poland, and Hungary. Essays in English and Russian.

343. Shapiro, Jane P., and Peter J. Potichnyj (eds.) (1976). *Change and Adaptation in Soviet and East European Politics*. New York: Praeger. Annotations, xii + 236pp.

Twelve essays presented at the First International Slavic Conference held in Banff, Alberta, Canada in September, 1974. Key issues include rapid social change, modernization and industrialization, and political leadership in Poland, Hungary, Czechoslovakia, Bulgaria, the U.S.S.R., and Central Asia. Part 1 examines communist political culture, Part 2 discusses censorship control, and Part 3 addresses multinational state conflicts.

344. Shelley, Louise (1979). "Soviet and Yugoslavian Criminology," *International Journal of Comparative and Applied Criminal Justice*, 3(2): 143-156. Bibliography.

Compares post-World War II Soviet and Yugoslavian criminology. Traces the condition of criminology in both countries -- historical background, geography, education, analytical sophistication, and research. Suggests that differences in the respective national criminologies derive from each country's specific history, degree of freedom in and commitment to research, and structure and organization.

345. Shelley, Louise (1980). "Crime and Delinquency in the Soviet Union." Pp.208-226 in Jerry G. Pankhurst and Michael Paul Sacks (eds.), *Contemporary Soviet Society: Sociological Perspectives*. New York: Praeger. Bibliography.

Examines the relationships among economic development, migration, and crime and delinquency in the U.S.S.R. Compares unique Soviet crime patterns with the industrialized communities of North, Siberia, the Far East, and Bulgaria. Discusses how and why Soviet crime patterns differ from most industrialized nations and identifies social characteristics of offenders. Provides conviction rates for economic, personal, and property crimes circa 1960 and 1976 and recidivism rates of murderers and rapists during 1926-1966. Includes a review of Soviet and Western theories of crime.

346. Shelley, Louise I. (1981). "Urbanization and Crime: The Soviet Case in Cross-Cultural Perspective." Pp.141-152 in Louise I. Shelley (ed.), *Readings in Comparative Criminology*. Carbondale, Illinois: Southern Illinois University Press. Annotations.

Examines the relationships among urbanization, population mobilization, migration patterns, and nonpolitical crime in the U.S.S.R. Includes crime data analysis and positions findings in a cross-cultural context. Argues that the U.S.S.R. has redistributed its major crime problems from its large cities to medium-size cities and rural areas.

347. Shelley, Louise I. (1981). *Crime and Modernization: The Impact of Industrialization and Urbanization on Crime*. Carbondale:: Southern Illinois University Press. Bibliography, xxii + 186pp.

Investigates historical influence of modernization, rapid social change, and socioeconomic development on crime patterns. A unilinear concept of 'modernization' is used as a key to unlock these relationships. Three distinct types of society are examined: developed capitalist countries, undeveloped capitalist countries, and socialist countries.

348. Shikita, Minoru (1985). "Violence and Urbanization: The Experience of Large Japanese Cities." Pp.661-674 in Pedro R. David (ed.), *Crime and Criminal Policy*. Pub. 25. Milan: United Nations Social Defence Research Institute.

Reviews official aggregate crime rates for larger Japanese cities and compares these with those of cities in other countries for 1978. Cities include New York, Tokyo, London, Paris, Los Angeles, West Berlin, Chicago, Yokohama, and Osaka. Crimes include murder, robbery, bodily injury, rape, and larceny. Discussion offers various explanations for

Japan's low crime rate and the difference between rural and urban crime rates. Addresses problems with official crime data.

349. Smykla, John Ortiz (1989). "Placing Uruguayan Corrections in Context, 1973-1984: A Note on the Visiting Criminologist's Role," *Journal of Criminal Justice*, 17(1): 25-37. Bibliography.

Describes the history of Uruguay's cultural and political structures and the relationship between the correctional system and political dictatorship from 1973 to 1984. Reviews theories used in comparative analysis. Provides arrest and disposition rates for juvenile offenses and offenders during 1981-1984. Includes a discussion of the difficulties encountered by the author during his field research.

350. Spitzer, Steven (1979). "Notes Toward a Theory of Punishment and Social Change," *Research in Law and Sociology* (eds. Rita J. Simon and Steven Spitzer, Greenwich, Connecticut: JAI Press), 2: 207-229. Notes, bibliography.

Critically outlines four hypotheses in order to advance a theory of punishment and social change which yields to historical and comparative inquiry. Hypotheses include 'organic differentiation', 'political centralization', 'political legitimacy', and 'labor control.' Provides a review of problems in the conceptualization of legal coercion and social development.

351. Sumner, Colin (ed.) (1982). *Crime, Justice and Underdevelopment*. London: Macmillan. Notes, bibliography, xvi + 345pp.

An important collection of nine essays on the relationship in Third World nations between imperialism and underdevelopment and between crime and justice. Areas addressed include Tanganyika, Senegal, and Nairobi in Africa; Cali, Colombia; Papua New Guinea; and Cuba. Authors address, from a variety of Marxist perspectives, the historical and legal processes whereby capitalism and colonialism create and perpetuate a distinct set of crimes and social harms. Sumner's introduction is a useful corrective to the ethnocentrism of much comparative criminology.

352. Taylor, Ian (1983). *Crime, Capitalism and Commumunity: Three essays in socialist criminology*. Toronto: Butterworths. Notes, bibliography, xi + 156pp.

Contains three essays, each originally written during 1979-1980 and then rewritten for thematic unity here. Critical themes include a popular criminology for Canada, homicide and violence in Canada, and expenditure and restructuring of the Canadian state. Contains numerous comparisons between Canadian and British criminology and criminal justice.

353. Van Den Berg, Ger P. (1985). *The Soviet System of Justice: Figures and Policy*. Dordrecht, the Netherlands: Martinus Nijhoff. Bibliography, 374pp.

An analysis of Soviet crime statistics, several categories of crime (crimes against the state, ownership, the person, public order, and administration of justice; official crime; economic crime; and petty crime), sentencing policies, corrective labor camps and forced labor from

1920s to mid 1970s. Contains occasional explicit comparisons among the U.S.S.R., other socialist countries, and the U.S. Four appendices cover demographic data, civil law, and arbitration statistics, and criminal law statistics.

354. Volgyes, Ivan (1978) (ed.). *Social Deviance in Eastern Europe*. Boulder, Colorado: Westview Press. Annotations, xv + 198pp.

Contains eight articles on contemporary forms of social deviance (economic, social, and political) in Czechoslovakia, Hungary, Poland, Romania, and Yugoslavia. Forms of deviance examined include prostitution, alcoholism, bribery and corruption, and the private economy. Discusses official and cultural concepts and range of deviance. Reviews Western theories of social deviance.

355. Weisser, Michael R. (1979). *Crime and Punishment in Early Modern Europe*. Atlantic Highlands, New Jersey: Humanities Press. Notes, bibliography, xi + 193pp.

Traces historical and cultural changes in crime and punishment in Europe during the transition from feudalism to industrialization. Countries include England, France, Italy, and Spain. Includes crimes against individuals and property offenses, rural and urban dimensions, class and social relations, and sanction methods. Chapter 9 is a summary comparative discussion.

356. Wellford, Charles F. (1974). "Crime and the Dimensions of Nations," *International Journal of Criminology and Penology*, 2(1): 1-10. Notes, bibliography.

Employs Interpol data and Dimensions of Nations project data to compare the relationship between national characteristics (e.g., industrialization and social change) and crime. Outlines methodology which tests for a number of crimes including homicide, sex offenses, major/minor larceny, fraud, counterfeiting, and drug abuse. Reviews relevant criminological literature.

357. Wolf, Preben (1971). "Crime and Development. An International Comparison of Crime Rates," *Scandinavian Studies in Criminology*, 3: 107-120. Bibliography.

Compares levels of crime in 25 countries from 1958 to 1964. Uses Interpol data for 1962-1969 and Uniform Crime Reports (UCR) data for 1958-1962. Crimes studied include willful murder, major and minor larceny, sex offenses, fraud, counterfeiting, drug offenses, and miscellaneous offenses. Discusses methodological problems, crime trends, and the relationship between crime and social development.

358. Zehr, Howard (1976). *Crime and the Development of Modern Society: Patterns of Criminality in Nineteenth-Century Germany and France*. London: CroomHelm. Bibliography, 188pp.

An influential macro-level comparative analysis of sociohistorical crime trends and rates in nineteenth-century Germany and France. Focus is the empirical investigation of urban and rural crime and the relationships among modernization, industrialization, economic environment, and crime patterns.

359. Zehr, Howard (1981). "The Modernization of Crime in Germany and France, 1830-1913." Pp.120-140 in Louise I. Shelley (ed.), *Readings in Comparative Criminology*. Carbondale, Illinois: Southern Illinois University Press. Annotations.

Examines crime trends and crime rates, and the relationship between modernization and crime, in urban and rural Germany and France between 1830 and 1913. Uses official police data to investigate crimes of theft and assault and battery. Provides crime and conviction ratios for both countries.

PART III

SOCIAL CONTROL AND CRIMINAL JUSTICE

10

Social Control and Dispute Resolution

360. Abel, Richard L. (ed.) (1982). *The Politics of Informal Justice, Volume 2: Comparative Studies*. New York: Academic Press. Bibliographies, x + 338pp.

Ten essays that address the diverse institutions and ideologies of informal justice in a variety of historical and contemporary societies. Types of society include nonindustrial, Third World, precapitalist, liberal capitalist, prefascist, and socialist. Studies refer to India, Germany and Japan in the 1920s and 1930s, Argentina, Allende's Chile, Portugal, and Mozambique.

361. Abraham, Henry J. (1986). *The Judicial Process: An Introductory Analysis of the Courts of the United States, England and France*. New York: Oxford University Press. Notes, bibliography, appendices, xiv + 624pp.

Offers a comparative introduction to the judicial process in the U.S., England and Wales, and France. Outlines the institutional and administrative features of judicial procedure. Discusses legal definitions and concepts, i.e., public and private law, court staff, and their qualifications and authorization.

362. Barnum, David G. (1987). "Constitutional Organization and the Protection of Human Rights in Britain and the United States." Pp.183-199 in John R. Schmidhauser (ed.), *Comparative Judicial Systems: Challenging Frontiers in Conceptual and Empirical Analysis*. London: Butterworths. Notes, bibliography.

Examines the organization of the British and U.S. constitutions and their consequences for the safeguarding and preservation of human rights. Critically reviews British and U.S. constitutional organization and attempts to broaden the legal scope of their effects.

363. Becker, Theodore L. (1987). *Comparative Judicial Politics: The Political Functionings of Courts*. Lanham, Maryland: University Press of America. Notes, appendices, xvi + 407pp.

Seeks to reconceptualize political inquiry and process through the comparative analysis of judicial systems and their structures, procedures philosophies, and roles. Appendices review various court cases in England, the U.S., Pakistan, the Philippines, India, West Germany, and Japan.

364. Bergesen, Albert (1984). "Social Control and Corporate Organization: A Durkheimian Perspective." Pp.141-170 in vol.2 of Donald Black (ed.), *Toward a General Theory of Social Control*. 2 vols. Orlando, Florida: Academic Press. Notes, bibliography.

Pursues a Durkheimian analysis of the social functions of crime and religious ritual in maintaining social solidarity. Uses examples from the U.S., Maoist China, and countries with Anglo-American style pluralist governments, to uncover the processes in which political witchhunts unfold even though no crime has been committed.

365. Bianchi, Herman, Mario Simondi, and Ian Taylor (eds.) (1975). *Deviance and Control in Europe*. London: John Wiley. Notes, bibliographies, xxiii + 209pp.

Fifteen essays from the European Group for the Study of Deviance and Social Control, plus notes and comments. Topics include national reports on criminology in Britain, Italy, The Netherlands, West Germany, and Norway; prison movements in Scandinavia, Britain, France, and Italy; and selected essays on criminal organization, criminal law, psychiatric control, and blackmail.

366. Black, Donald (1976). *The Behavior of Law*. New York; Academic Press. Bibliography, xi + 175pp.

A much-debated scientific theory of law (defined as 'governmental social control') in which the style and quantity of law is seen to vary with stratification, morphology, culture, social organization, and social control. Explicit crosscultural and historical analyses are profusely illustrated. Contains several comparative propositions about the definition of crime and the operation of criminal justice.

367. Black, Donald (ed.) (1984). *Toward a General Theory of Social Control*. 2 vols. Orlando, Florida: Academic Press. Notes, bibliographies.

Volume 1 ('Fundamentals') contains eleven essays on the basic principles of social control in a variety of cultures and periods. Volume 2 ('Selected Problems') contains eleven essays on selected problems in social control.

368. Black, Donald (1984). "Crime as Social Control." Pp.1-27 in vol.2 of Donald Black (ed.), *Toward a General Theory of Social Control*. 2 vols. Orlando, Florida: Academic Press. Notes, bibliography.

Draws attention to the ways in which many crimes operate as forms of social control. Argues that much crime is moralistic, pursues justice, is a form of conflict management, and possibly a form of punishment. Tries to explain and predict crime through a sociological theory of self-help. Numerous cross-cultural generalizations about crimes, especially homicide.

369. Dupuy, Pierre-Marie (1989). "Implications of the Institutionalization of International Crimes of State." Pp.170-185 in Joseph H.H. Weiler, Antonio Cassese and Marina Spinedi (eds.), *International Crimes of State: A Critical Analysis of the ILC's Draft Article on State Responsibility.* Berlin: Walter de Gruyter. Annotations.

Summarizes the advantages and dangers of incorporating systematized state responsibility within the rules of international law. Discusses the legal distinctions between (1) international crimes and delicts, (2) the effects of institutionalized obligation and legal responsibility and, (3) the possible risk of inconsistent implementation. Offers procedural recommendations to ensure successful application of international law.

370. Edwards, Anne (1988). *Regulation and Repression: the Study of Social Control.* Sydney: Allen & Unwin. Notes, bibliography, v + 281pp.

Criticizes existing sociological, radical, and feminist theories of social control. Outlines historical and comparative trends and shifts in patterns of social control in Australia, Britain, and U.S. from 18th century to present. Examines in depth legal-judicial, medical-psychiatric, and social welfare systems.

371. Ehrmann, Henry W. (1976). *Comparative Legal Cultures.* Englewood Cliffs, New Jersey: Prentice Hall. Notes, bibliography, xv + 172pp.

A functional approach combining various political, sociological, and philosophical aspects with the comparative study of law. Analyses the effects of law and legal institutions on the individual and society. Discusses judicial procedures, decision-making processes, legal limitations, and historical and contemporary legal matters. Offers litigation rates for a variety of countries including: Australia, Denmark, Sweden, Finland, New Zealand, Britain, and Japan.

372. Figueira-McDonough, Josefina (1979). "Processing Juvenile Delinquency in Two Cities: A Cross National Comparison," *Journal of Research in Crime and Delinquency*, 16(1): 114-142. Notes, bibliography.

A comparison of juvenile court systems in the U.S. city of 'Metro' and the Brazilian city of Rio de Janeiro. Both court systems function in similar large metropolitan environments with similar ecological profiles. Finds that U.S. courts process ten times more juveniles than Brazilian courts and that courts which process large numbers of cases tend to become alienated from their original concern with goals such as justice.

373. Gaja, Giorgio (1989). "Obligations *Erga Omnes*, International Crimes and *Jus Cogens*: A Tentative Analysis of Three Related Concepts." Pp.151-160 in Joseph H.H. Weiler, Antonio Cassese, and Marina Spinedi (eds.), *International Crimes of State: A Critical Analysis of the ILC's Draft Article on State Responsibility.* Berlin: Walter de Gruyter. Annotations.

Critically examines the legal concepts *erga omnes* (state obligations) and *jus cogens* (peremptory norms) and their relationship to state obligations for international crimes of state. Reviews international legal cases in order to demonstrate interpretation and application of concepts discussed.

374. Garth, Bryant (1982). "The Movement toward Procedural Informalism in North America and Western Europe: A Critical Survey." Pp.183-211 in Richard L. Abel (ed.), *The Politics of Informal Justice, Volume 2: Comparative Studies*. New York: Academic Press. Bibliography.

Examines the historical relationship between aspects of law in the welfare state and procedural informalism in the U.S. and in Britain, France, and The Netherlands. Discusses the decline of procedural formalism, the evolution of the legal and judicial process of procedural informalism, and differences between European and U.S. welfare institutions and their movement toward procedural informalism.

375. Glos, George E. (1979). *Comparative Law*. Littleton, Colorado: Fred B. Rothman. Annotations, appendix, xxxv + 787pp.

A comprehensive cross-cultural view of the essential features of civil, criminal, and administrative law in various countries, including France, Germany, Italy, and Spain. Discusses laws which pertain to court officials. Includes case reviews and decisions with comparative utility and legal annotations for Austria, Switzerland, and Mexico.

376. Gluckman, Max (1959). "The Technical Vocabulary of Barotse Jurisprudence," *American Anthropologist*, 61(6, part 2): 743-759. Bibliography.

Investigates the legal language and conceptualization of Barotse jurisprudence, and its operative features regarding the structure of land ownership. Examines the complex relationships among social structure, relative status, and legal rights and obligations.

377. Gulliver, P.H. (1979). *Disputes and Negotiations: A Cross-Cultural Perspective*. New York: Academic Press. Notes, bibliography, xxi + 293pp.

Attempts to show that patterns of interaction in negotiations are basically similar despite marked differences in interests, ideas, values, rules, and assumptions among negotiators in different societies. Author draws on his research on negotiation in East Africa for comparisons of negotiation processes with Western societies. Chapter 8 compares a dispute between neighbors in Arusha with an industrial dispute in the U.S.

378. Haraszti, Gyorgy (1978). " The Comparative Method in International Law." Pp.311-321 in Imre Szabo and Zoltan Peteri (eds.), *Comparative Law*. Budapest: Akademiai Kiado. Annotations.

Discusses the application of comparative methodology to international law. Focus is the different objectives in the comparative study of international and municipal law. Discusses problems of methodological interpretation of international law, comparative law, municipalities and treaties, and the advancement of new international legal norms. Suggests that international law is a legal system of its own.

379. Harnett, Catherine M., and Richard H. Anson (1982). "Legal Diversity in the Middle East: Some Comparative Research Horizons," *International Journal of Comparative and Applied Criminal Justice*, 6(1): 99-103. Bibliography.

Seeks to encourage academic interest in comparative criminal justice systems. Traces the historical processes of Middle Eastern legal philosophy and the ascendancy of Islamic rule which led to the culmination of distinct types of jurisprudence.

380. Hazard, John N. (1969). *Communists and Their Law: A Search for the Common Core of the Legal Systems of the Marxian Socialist States*. Chicago: University of Chicago Press. Notes, bibliography, xvi + 560pp.

Chapter 16 ('Correction of Criminals in a Renovating Society') and Chapter 17 ('Types of Crime in the Absence of Capitalism') contain selected discussion and comparison of crime and criminal justice institutions in the U.S.S.R., Eastern European communist countries, Cuba, and China.

381. Humphries, Drew, and David F. Greenberg (1984). "Social Control and Social Formation: A Marxian Analysis." Pp.171-208 in vol.2 of Donald Black (ed.), *Toward a General Theory of Social Control*. 2 vols. Orlando, Florida: Academic Press. Notes, bibliography.

Shows how Marxism can contribute to a general theory of social control. Includes discussion of capital's puritannical regulation of desire, and of the relationship among industrial capitalism and the police, proportionality in punishment, and the penitentiary.

382. Kidder, Robert L. (1988). "Finding Our Voice in Japan: Upham's Law and Social Change in Japan," *Law & Social Inquiry*, 13(2): 407-412. Annotations.

Reviews Upham's *Law and Social Change in Postwar Japan* [see # 412]. Discusses Upham's thesis about the effectiveness of informal legal and political control strategies. Suggests that Upham's book provides the start for a cliché-free generation of comparative research on Japanese and U.S. legal systems.

383. Krase, Jerome and Edward Sagarin (1980). "Formal and Informal Social Control In Cross-Cultural Perspective." Pp.211-235 in Graeme R. Newman (ed.), *Crime and Deviance: A Comparative Perspective*. Beverly Hills, California: Sage. Bibliography.

Addresses the importance of informal social control systems and their relationship to formal agencies of control and sanctions. Discusses sexuality and alcoholism as topical issues in order to demonstrate systematic cross-cultural differences and trends in developed and developing nations. The developed nations include Japan, China, and the U.S.S.R.; developing countries include Africa and Mexico.

384. Jan, Lee-Jan (1983). "Deterrence as Social Control in the United States and China," *International Journal of Comparative and Applied Criminal Justice*, 7(2): 195-200. Bibliography.

Compares methods of deterrence used to control deviant opinion and behavior in the U.S. and China. Outlines U.S. and Chinese social control philosophies, models, and trends. Discusses the advantages and limitations of both models. Findings suggest that the U.S. often relies on external constraints, while China emphasizes internal restrictions.

385. Jescheck, Hans-Heinrich (1970). "Principles of German Criminal Procedure in Comparison with American Law," *Virginia Law Review*, 56(2): 239-253. Annotations.

Outlines and compares criminal procedure in the U.S. and Germany. Discusses constitutional law (the preservation of human rights), truth discoveries and their presentation, jury trials, the role of the judge, defendant's position at trial, and the organization and function of the public prosecutor's office. Reviews problems and developments in Germany's criminal procedure.

386. Liebesny, Herbert J. (1981). *Foreign Legal Systems: A Comparative Analysis*. Washington, D.C.: George Washington University. Appendices, xi + 413pp.

Compares various legal systems with particular emphasis on civil/common law. Discusses historical origins, criminal law and procedure, statute interpretation, the legal profession, judicial and procedural concepts, and legal reforms. Countries discussed include Germany, France, Italy, Belgium, The Netherlands, Portugal, Egypt, Turkey, Iran, India, Pakistan, Austria, and Switzerland. Includes a review of legal cases.

387. Little, Craig B. (1984). "Deviance, Social Control and the Origins of Legitimacy in England and the United States," *Research in Law, Deviance and Social Control* (ed. Steven Spitzer and Andrew T. Scull, Greenwich, Connecticut: JAI Press), 6: 57-78. Notes, bibliography.

Examines the different bases on which deviance, legitimacy, and social control were constituted in England and the U.S. Key differences hinge on the respective ways in which their bourgeois revolutions were resolved, the rise of popular government, nature of early working-class discontent, and development of mass consumer culture.

388. Madl, Ferenc (1978). "A Comparative Law Theory on Developing Norms in Private International Law." Pp.85-106 in Imre Szabo and Zoltan Peteri (eds.), *Comparative Law*. Budapest: Akademiai Kiado. Annotations.

A theoretical approach to the study of comparative private international law that tests theoretical concepts of the institutions of renvoi, reciprocity, and torts. Outlines two premises of comparative private international law: (1) the relevance of positive law, and (2) reliance on institutions of substantive law. Focuses on the conceptual requirements of a theoretical approach, the relationship between society and law, the 'reality-oriented' legal science approach, and the problems facing a comprehenisve theory of private international law.

389. McDonald, Lynn (1976). *The Sociology of Law and Order*. Boulder, Colorado: Westview Press. Notes, bibliography, 340pp.

Uses Interpol data, United Nations juvenile court data, and British and Canadian official crime statistics to test a variety of theories about the causes of crime. Challenges the view that serious crimes rose rapidly in the 1960s and 1970s. Major themes include 'general theories of crime, law, and sanctions,' 'testing general theories,' and 'the state of the subject' (the sociology of law and order).

390. Merry, Sally Engle (1982). "The Social Organization of Mediation in Nonindustrial Societies: Implications for Informal Community Justice in America." Pp.17-45 in Richard L. Abel (ed.), *The Politics of Informal Justice, Volume 2 : Comparative Studies*. New York: Academic Press. Bibliography.

Examines mediation as a mode of settling disputes in various small-scale horticultural and pastoral societies, including the Nuer, the Arusha and Ndendeuli, the Tiv, the Ifugao, the Tongo, the Cheyenne, the Swat Pathan and Waigali, Sardinian shepherds, Zambia, Mexico, Taiwan, Italy, Japan, Lebanon, and Liberian peasant villagers. Discusses how mediation is limited by type of social organization, and identifies problems of applying it to highly industrialized societies such as the U.S.

391. Michalowski, Raymond J. (1985). *Order, Law, and Crime: An Introduction to Criminology*. New York: Random House. Annotations, xiii + 422pp.

An introductory criminology textbook whose comparative features are accessible to those with only limited knowledge of the field. Chapter 3 outlines the anthropological concern with order, trouble, deviance, and conformity in acephelous societies. Refers to a variety of simple societies, including the Nuer, Eskimos, Ifugao, Semai, and Tiwi.

392. Moore, Sally Falk (1978). *Law as Process: An Anthropological Approach*. London: Routledge & Kegan Paul. Bibliography, 270pp.

An integrated series of essays that address the evolutionary process of law. Traces development and transformation of legal systems from early to contemporary societies. Discusses anthropological approach to legal analysis. Proposes a framework for social and cultural study. Chapter 4 reviews anthropology of law literature.

393. Moore, Wilbert E. and Joyce Sterling (1985). "The Comparison of Legal Systems: A Critique," *Quaderni Fiorentini*, 14: 77-117. Bibliography.

Theoretically explores the meaning and definition of law, the possibile universality of law, and various ways of comparing legal systems. Criticizes several theories of law, including Marxism, neo-evolutionism and functionalism. Reviews several theoretical and methodological concepts of comparative law.

394. Nader, Laura (1965). "The Anthropological Study of Law," *American Anthropologist*, 67(6, part 2): 3 32. Notes, bibliography.

An important essay asking "What is law?" Summarises some major anthropological propositions and inquiries about law. Discusses relevant sociological and anthropological literature, and current anthropological approaches to the study of law. Outlines historical and cross-cultural characteristics of law.

395. Nader, Laura, and Harry F. Todd Jr. (eds.) (1978). *The Disputing Process. Law in Ten Societies.* New York: Columbia University Press. Bibliography, xx + 372.

An influential collection of 10 anthropological essays on disputes and the organizational and structural processes of resolution in the New Guinea Highlands, a Bavarian village, a Turkish village, Shehaam, Lebanon, and a Sunni Muslim village in Lebanon, urban Ghana, Zambia, Sardinia, a Mexican district, and Rock Island. Examines law as a function item of social process, methodological and theoretical framework, and ethnographic features.

396. Porter, Jack Nusan (1982). *Conflict and Conflict Resolution: A Historical Bibliography.* New York: Garland Publishing. xiii + 115pp.

Annotated historical bibliography of conflict and conflict resolution. Contains chapters on reference sources, classical nineteenth-century theorists, twentieth-century theorists, contemporary general works, conflict resolution, and journals, newsletters, and annuals.

397. Pospisil, Leopold (1971). *Anthropology of Law: A Comparative Theory.* New York: Harper & Row. Bibliography, xiii + 385pp.

Offers a systematic anthropological theory of law ('procedure') based on author's study of Hopi Indians in Arizona, the Kapauku Papuans of West New Guinea, and the Nunamiut Eskimos of Alaska. Outlines the basis for a definition of law. Discusses legal forms, attributes of law, multiplicity of legal systems, changes in law and legal systems, justice, and substantive law.

398. Ratner, R.S., and John L. McMullan (1983). "Social Control and the Rise of the 'Exceptional State' in Britain, the United States, and Canada," *Crime and Social Justice*, 19: 31-43. Bibliography.

Examines the ways in which the New Right has mobilized crime, law, order, and punishment for ideological purposes. Discusses criminal justice politics and the rise of 'exceptional states' in Britain, the U.S., and Canada during the mid 1970s to early 1980s.

399. Roberts, Simon (1979). *Order and Dispute: An Introduction to Legal Anthropology.* New York: St. Martin's Press. Bibliography, 216pp.

An introduction to the diverse ways in which small-scale simple societies keep order and resolve disputes without centralized systems of social control. Reviews history of legal anthropology, including such concepts as law, rules, dispute, dispute-settlement processes, and state and stateless societies.

400. Rueschemeyer, Dietrich (1978). "The Legal Profession in Comparative Perspective." Pp.97-127 in Harry M. Johnson (ed.), *Social System and Legal Process.* San Francisco, California: Jossey-Bass. Notes, bibliography.

A comparative review of the legal profession in the U.K., Japan, Germany, and the U.S. between 1960 and 1961. Discusses the historical development of legal norms, legal systems, and legal procedures in various societies, including developed and developing nations such as Kenya, Nigeria, and Sierra Leone. Describes cultural differences and the role and scope of law and legal counsellors in contemporary societies.

401. Saney, Parviz (1986). *Crime and Culture in America: A Comparative Perspective.* Westport, Connecticut: Greenwood Press. Notes, bibliography, 215pp.

An eclectic book that focuses on the relationships between the social, institutional, and political aspects of culture and their diverse effects both on various social control systems and on criminal activity in the U.S. Compares crime trends in the U.S. with other industrialized countries such as France, The Netherlands, Sweden, Italy, Denmark, Germany, Austria, and Japan.

402. Schichor, David, and John W. Heeren (1989). "Social Control in Socialist Societies: An Analysis of Five Major Characteristics," *Legal Studies Forum*, 13(3): 215-238. Notes, bibliography.

Authors' intent is to analyze the 'common core' characteristics of formal social control mechanisms in socialist societies up to the mid-1980s. Characteristics include those associated with crime control, politicization, rehabilitation and reeducation, pervasiveness, and mass participation. Recommends further study of any convergence in the criminal justice policies of socialist and capitalist-democratic societies.

403. Schmidhauser, John R. (ed.) (1987). *Comparative Judicial Systems: Challenging Frontiers in Conceptual and Empirical Analysis.* London: Butterworths. Notes, bibliography, 243pp.

A series of comparative and abstract analyses focusing on systems of judicial process. Part 1 describes comparative frameworks and their developmental problems. Part 2 consists of several single culture analyses of Canada, Israel, India, England, and Germany. Part 3 examines judicial systems in England, the U.S., and Japan.

404. Schubert, Glendon (1987). "Subcultures and Judicial Background: A Cross-Cultural Analysis." Pp.222-239 in John R. Schmidhauser (ed.), *Comparative Judicial Systems: Challenging Frontiers in Conceptual and Empirical Analysis.* London: Butterworths. Bibliography.

Compares subcultural differences between Swiss and South African Supreme Court judges. Utilizes cross-sectional survey data for comparative analysis of the relationships among judicial attributes, attitudes, and decision-making. Offers a partial methodological design which reviews control variables.

405. Schubert, Glendon, and David J. Danelski (eds.) (1969). *Comparative Judicial Behavior: Cross Cultural Studies of Political Decision-Making in the East and West.* London: Oxford University Press. Annotations, xxii + 412pp.

Fourteen single-culture essays that focus on various aspects of judicial behavior in Korea, Japan, the Philippines, Hawaii, India, Canada, and Australia. Essays examine judicial decision-making process, including judicial attitudes and procedures.

406. Schwartz, Richard (1954). "Social Factors in the Development of Legal Control: A Case Study of Two Israeli Settlements," *Yale Law Journal*, 63(4): 471 491. Annotations.

Examines the relationship between economic collectivism and formal and informal social control mechanisms in Israeli Kvutza and Moshav settlement communities. Outlines theoretical propositions, legal procedures, and systematic social control differences and their effects.

407. Snyder, Francis G. (1981). "Anthropology, Dispute Processes and Law: A Critical Introduction," *British Journal of Law and Society*, 8(2): 141-180. Notes, bibliography.

Outlines some of the main themes of current anthropological studies of law and dispute processes. Critically reviews development of anthropology and its contribution to the sociology of law derived from U.S., British, and European literature.

408. Soothill, K.L., *et al.* (1981). "Social Control of Deviants in Six Countries," *Medicine, Science and Law*, 21(1): 31-40. Bibliography.

Part of a World Health Organization research project, this study compares networks of social control in Brazil, Denmark, Egypt, Swaziland, Switzerland, and Thailand. Discusses differences between the formal social control systems of health and criminal justice. Outlines various stages of the social control process, including discovery, official screening, disposal, release and aftercare.

409. Spinedi, Marina (1989). "International Crimes of State: The Legislative History." Pp.7-138 in Joseph H.H. Weiler, Antonio Cassese, and Marina Spinedi (eds.), *International Crimes of State: A Critical Analysis of the ILC's Draft Article 19 on State Responsibility*. Berlin: Walter de Gruyter. Annotations.

Part 1 reviews the legislative origin, content, codification, and possible intention and interpretation of the United Nations Draft Article 19 on International Crimes of State and International Delicts. Discusses various state opinions of Draft Article 19 and the International Law Commission's preparatory work. Part 2 addresses Draft Article 19's major conceptual difficulties in relation to state responsibility in International Crimes of State.

410. Spitzer, Steven (1982). "The Dialectics of Formal and Informal Control." Pp.167-205 in Richard L. Abel (ed.), *The Politics of Informal Justice, Volume 1 : The American Experience*. New York: Academic Press. Bibliography.

Written from a radical perspective on the 1970s delegalization movement, this essay examines the dialectical character of formal and informal social control in precapitalist and capitalist societies. Comments on the contradictions, ironies, and complexities of popular justice; People's Republic of China is a case study.

411. Tate, Neal C. (1987). "Judicial Institutions in Cross-National Perspective: Toward Integrating Courts into the Comparative Study of Politics." Pp.7-33 in John R. Schmidhauser (ed.), *Comparative Judicial Systems: Challenging Frontiers in*

Conceptual and Empirical Analysis. London: Butterworths. Notes, bibliography.

Argues for the comparative integration of judicial and political analysis. Focus is the political and institutional roles of courts. Outlines data sources employable in comparative political theory construction, and critically reviews several conceptual frameworks in comparative government and politics, in public law and judicial process, and in sources outside political science.

412. Upham, Frank J. (1987). *Law and Social Change in Postwar Japan*. Cambridge, Massachusetts: Harvard University Press. Notes, bibliography, x + 269pp.

Focuses on the postwar relationships among social structure, culture, ideology, and the legal system in Japan. Shows how legal informalism operates in a rapidly changing and complex industrial society. Examines environmental pollution, civil rights violations against the Burakumin, the movement for equal employment opportunities for women, and anti-monopoly policy struggles in the 1980s. Chapter 6 contains explicit comparisons of Japanese and U.S. perspectives.

413. Waltman, Jerold L., and Kenneth M. Holland (eds.) (1988). *The Political Role of Law Courts in Modern Democracies*. New York: St. Martin's Press. Annotations, ix + 237pp.

Eleven single culture essays on the political process of judicial change in democracies such as the U.S., Australia, Canada, the Federal Republic of Germany, England, France, Italy, Sweden, and Japan. Essays address distinct structural and functional aspects of law courts. Final chapter discusses the relationships among courts, political change, and post industrial society.

414. Wolfe, Nancy Travis (1983). "Participation in Courts: American Jurors and German Lay Judges." Pp.121-134 in Israel L. Barak-Glantz and Elmer H. Johnson (eds.), *Comparative Criminology*. Beverly Hills, California: Sage. Notes, bibliography.

Compares the responsibilities and judicial patterns of behavior of U.S. petit jurors and German lay judges. Focuses on variations in judicial and juror participation. Reviews relevant juror research studies and findings.

11

Criminal Justice and Penal Policies

415. Akers, Ronald L., Norman S. Hayner, and Werner Gruninger (1977). "Prisonization in Five Countries: Type of Prison and Inmate Characteristics," *Criminology*, 14(4): 527-554. Bibliography.

Uses random survey data to compare organizational and inmate characteristics in five prisons located in the U.S., Mexico, England, West Germany, and Spain. Examines inmate attitudes, criminal history, prison type, and staff interaction. Tests for functional and importation theories. Findings support functional model of inmate system.

416. Akers, Ronald, Werner Gruninger, and Norman S. Hayner (1976). "Prison Inmate Roles: Inter-organizational and Cross-Cultural Comparisons," *International Journal of Criminology and Penology*, 4(4): 365-381. Notes, bibliography.

Employs interview data and cross-cultural data derived from a previous study in order to interpret the interorganizational and functional characteristics of prison and inmate behavior in the U.S., West Germany, England, and Spain. Discusses methodological limitations. Reviews and tests importation and functional theories of correctional institutions. Methodological design detailed. Findings support importation model.

417. Ahlstrom-Laakso, Salme (1971). "Arrests for Drunkenness: Two Capital Cities," *Scandinavian Studies in Criminology*, 3: 89-105. Bibliography.

Examines the social control factors that contribute to different arrest rates for drunkenness in Helsinki (Finland) and Copenhagen (Denmark). Discusses formal and informal social control processes and arrest rates, community values, structural aspects of inebriation and arrest, and research problems. Findings suggest that differences in social control systems, social values, and the presence of informal shelters and social gatherings, may contribute to different arrest rates.

418. Allen, Frederick G. (1987). "Reforming Criminals in China: Implications for Corrections in the West," *International Journal of Comparative and Applied Criminal Justice*, 11(1): 77-86. Annotations.

Outlines contemporary Chinese legal concepts and discusses their allegedly humane rehabilitative penal process. Reviews discussant's visits to three Chinese prisons where observations and official interviews were conducted. Reviews East/West judicial and correctional differences. Some recidivism rates provided.

419. Anderson, Malcolm (1989). *Policing the World: Interpol and the Politics of International Police Co-operation.* Oxford: Clarendon Press. Notes, bibliography, x + 211pp.

A study of the parochial and nationalist difficulties facing Interpol's attempt to police the increasing problem of international crime. Chapters deal with the background, history and legal basis of Interpol in the world community; the evolving activities and functions of Interpol; the problems of drugs and terrorism; and bilateral and international police cooperation.

420. Bayley, David H. (1976). *Forces of Order: Police Behavior in Japan and the United States.* Berkeley, California: University of California Press. Annotations, xvi + 201pp.

Systematically compares procedural differences between Japanese and U.S. police institutions. Examines authoritative and organizational imperatives, societal violence, social control, and the communal role of the police. Methodology discussed.

421. Becker, Harold K. (1973). *Police Systems of Europe: A Survey of Selected Police Organizations.* Springfield, Illinois: Charles C. Thomas. Bibliography, appendices, xvi + 224pp.

Comparative investigation of the legal characteristics and political propensities of formal police systems. Focuses on the institutional structure and aspirations of various European police organizations in Austria, Belgium, France, West Germany, Italy, The Netherlands, Norway, Spain, and Sweden. Compares Copenhagen and Liverpool police systems.

422. Bennett, Richard R. (1982). "The Effect of Police Personnel Levels on Crime Clearance Rates: A Cross-National Analysis," *International Journal of Comparative and Applied Criminal Justice*, 6(2): 177-193. Notes, bibliography.

Explores the effect of police personnel levels of crime clearance. Uses regression analysis to control for selected structural factors in 60 countries, including (1) socio political, economic, and environmental conditions, (2) citizen-governmental conflict, and (3) the nature of crime. Uses Interpol data. Findings generally run counter to the assumption that police personnel levels have a positive effect on crime clearance rates.

423. Bensinger, Gad J. (1984). "Corrections in Israel and the United States: A Comparative Analysis," *International Journal*

of Comparative and Applied Criminal Justice, 8(1): 55-62. Bibliography.

Examines incarceration and probation as forms of judicial correction in Israel and the U.S. Discusses comparative institutional ideology, legal alternatives, Israel's substandard prison facilities, nationalized probationary assistance, and historical and structural features.

424. Bianchi, Herman, and Rene Van Swaaningen (eds.) (1986). *Abolitionism: Towards a Non-Repressive Approach to Crime.* Amsterdam: Free University Press. Notes, bibliographies, appendix, 247pp.

Twenty essays from the Second International Conference on Prison Abolition held in Amsterdam in 1985. Comprises a representative survey of the abolitionist movement, with authors from The Netherlands, Norway, Finland, Canada, England, the U.S., Israel, and the Federal Republic of Germany. Major themes include 'defining crime,' 'arguments for abolition,' 'the abolitionist perspective,' 'towards abolition,' and 'dispute settlement in practice.'

425. Bienvenue, Rita, and A.H. Latif (1975). "Arrests, Dispositions and Recidivism: A Comparison of Indians and Whites." Pp.355-367 in Robert A. Silverman and James J. Teevan (eds.), *Crime in Canadian Society.* Toronto: Butterworths. Annotations.

Utilizes official 1969 Canadian male/female arrest data to compare Indian and White groups. Includes comparisons of distribution rates for crimes against persons and property, judicial disposition, age, and gender delineation. Methodological design and discussion included.

426. Bossard, André (1990). *Transnational Crime and Criminal Law.* University of Illinois at Chicago: Office of International Criminal Justice. Notes, bibliography, vii + 155pp.

Written by the former Secretary General of the ICPO-Interpol, this book is based largely on Interpol data. Its seven chapters cover crimes against persons and property, international fraud, forgery and counterfeiting, smuggling and traffics, organized crime, and the response to transnational crime.

427. Boyd, Neil (1983). "Juvenile Release Programs in British Columbia and Ontario: A Comparative Analysis." Pp.303-314 in Raymond R. Corrado, Marc Leblanc, and Jean Trepanier (eds.), *Current Issues in Juvenile Justice.* Toronto: Butterworths. Annotations.

Compares juvenile release programs and policy changes in British Columbia and Ontario, Canada. Examines current juvenile release procedures, problems facing released delinquents and the political and organizational rationales of judicial decisions. Reviews relevant theoretical literature.

428. Braithwaite, John (1989). *Crime, Shame and Reintegration.* Cambridge: Cambridge University Press. Notes, bibliography, viii + 226pp.

Offers a general theory suggesting that the key to crime control lies in cultural commitments to shaming in 'reintegrative' ways. Addresses the social conditions and cultural contexts conducive to crime control through shaming. Finds control is powerful and efficient when shame accompanies respect for the offender. Theory tested with materials from ethnography, history, survey research, macrosociology, and experimental research designs. Comparative generalizations drawn from Japan, Britain, Australia, and the U.S.

429. Bratholm, Anders (1980). "Police Investigations and the Personal Integrity of the Suspect in Scandinavia," *Scandinavian Studies in Criminology*, 7: 107-123.

Critically discusses external and internal police investigative practices which violate law enforcement regulations and individual civil liberties in Norway, Denmark, and Sweden. Theoretically reviews Scandinavian laws and regulations and attempts to explain the inconsistencies between cultural ideals and reality regarding police investigative practices.

430. Brewer, John D., Adrian Guelke, Ian Hume, Edward Moxon-Browne, and Rick Wilford (1988). *The Police, Public Order and The State: Policing in Great Britain, Northern Ireland, the Irish Republic, the USA, Israel, South Africa and China*. New York: St. Martin's Press. Bibliography, xi + 245pp.

A comparative investigation of the structural, institutional, and functional duties associated with police administration, the political state, and public order. Provides a cross cultural description of the interchangeable role of the police as both arbitrators and managers of the status-quo. Countries examined include Britain, Northern Ireland, Ireland, the U.S., Israel, South Africa, and China.

431. Brusten, M., J. Graham, N. Herriger, and P. Malinowski (eds.) (1986). *Youth Crime, Social Control and Prevention: Theoretical Perspectives and Policy Implications*. Pfaffenweiler: Centaurus. Notes, bibliographies, x + 236pp.

Nineteen essays on youth crime and social control in North America, Japan, Nigeria, Israel, The Netherlands, Britain, West Germany, and Latin America. Topics include theoretical, conceptual, and critical perspectives; program evaluation; juvenile justice and criminal policy; and criminalization and criminal policy.

432. Bureau of Justice Statistics (1987). *Imprisonment in Four Countries*. Washington, D.C.: U.S. Department of Justice. NCJ-103967

Utilizes arrest data to estimate incarceration rates and discusses the probability of imprisonment for the crimes of robbery, burglary, and theft in the U.S., Canada, England, and the Federal Republic of Germany. Outlines methodological design. Discusses cross-cultural comparability. Excludes juvenile offenses.

433. Chang, Dae H. (1988). "Crime and Delinquency Control Strategy in Japan: A Comparative Note," *International Journal of Comparative and Applied Criminal Justice*, 12(2): 139-149. Bibliography.

Portrays features of Japan's criminal justice system which encourage low crime rates and compares these cultural factors with those found in the U.S. Discusses differences in law enforcement procedures, public cooperation, social structure, and worldview. Offers suggestions for reducing crime in the U.S.

434. Chappell, D., and P.R. Wilson (1969). *The Police and the Public in Australia and New Zealand.* Queensland: University of Queensland Press. Annotations, appendices, 214pp.

Employs survey data to compare police and public attitudes of each other in Australia and New Zealand. Contextually discusses historical developmental dimensions of Australian and New Zealand police organizations and contemporary problems facing these two police forces. Authors offer suggestions which may enhance police and public association.

435. Clarke, Michael (1990). "The Control of Insurance Fraud: a Comparative View," *British Journal of Criminology*, 30(1): 1-23. Bibliography.

Examines various responses to insurance fraud from the 1960s to the late 1980s in the U.S., Canada, France, Holland, West Germany, Britain, Ireland, and Italy. Finds that effective mechanisms of fraud control have common elements: insurers' willingness to share information and to form registers of aggravated risks; development of specialist expertise in detection and investigation; multi-stage construction of fraud awareness into insurance practices; use of publicity and propaganda; development and maintenance of research; and good relations with public authorities, especially fire and police services.

436. Cole, George F., Stanislaw J. Frankowski, and Marc G. Gertz (eds.) (1981). *Major Criminal Justice Systems.* Beverly Hills, California: Sage. Notes, bibliographies, 234pp.

Contains eight single culture chapters which provide information about the institutions, ideologies, and practices of three types of criminal justice system. Part 1 outlines the common law method of the U.S., England and Wales, and Canada. Part 2 describes civil law procedure in the Federal Republic of Germany, Sweden, and Japan. Part 3 discusses socialist law processes in Russia, Poland, and the German Democratic Republic.

437. Cooper, H.H.A. (1972). "Prison Problems in the USA and Peru," *International Journal of Offender Therapy and Comparative Criminology*, 16(1): 25-31. Bibliography.

Identifies and compares judicial and penitentiary problems in the U.S. and Peru. Focuses on cultural ideology, administrative legal features, problems and effects of contemporary correctional institutions and implementation, and rehabilitative success.

438. Currie, Elliott (1985) *Confronting Crime: An American Challenge.* New York: Pantheon. Annotations, viii + 326pp.

An important liberal text that addresses the causes of escalating crime rates in the U.S., especially violence. Explores ideologies of crime in the U.S. and the persistent and unsuccessful use of conservative state policies to reduce crime. Outlines structural and institutional welfare and employment policies that have been adopted in some European countries, such as Sweden, and which, the author suggests, would reduce crime if implemented in the U.S.

439. Dauber, Edward, and David Shichor (1979). "A Comparative Exploration of Prison Discipline," *Journal of Criminal Justice*, 7(1): 21-36. Notes, bibliography.

Investigates officially sanctioned correctional methods in Israel's Ramle prison and Rhode Island's State Prison. Discusses prison goals, judicial intervention, research methodology, and formal and informal disciplinary processes. Findings and interpretations are reviewed in comparative context.

440. Devine, Francis Edward (1986). "Detention Short of Arrest for Questioning: The United States, England, and Scotland," *International Journal of Comparative and Applied Criminal Justice*, 10(1): 57-72. Bibliography.

Examines legal status and common practices employed by officials when detaining individuals for interrogation in the U.S., England, and Scotland. Exemplifies several court cases which litigate questionable police detention practices in order to demonstrate the inherently ambiguous nature of law and legal process. Findings outline variations among countries studied.

441. Doleschal, Eugene (1977). "Rate and Length of Imprisonment: How Does the United States Compare with the Netherlands, Denmark and Sweden?" *Crime and Delinquency*, 23(1): 51-56. Annotations.

Critically discusses incarceration rates and sentencing range for The Netherlands, Denmark, and Sweden and compares their practices with those in the U.S. Outlines the methodological and institutional differences between the U.S., which adheres to a punitive rehabilitative mode, and The Netherlands, Denmark and Sweden, where greater leniency typically occurs.

442. Doleschal, Eugene, and Anne Newton (1979). *International Rates of Imprisonment*. Hackensack, New Jersey: National Council on Crime and Delinquency. 5pp.

An international report providing data about prison populations and incarceration rates in many countries for individuals sentenced and awaiting sentence as of January 1, 1974. Outlines incarceration rates and demographic data for the Republic of South Africa, U.S.S.R., U.S. (1977 and 1978), Britain (1976), West Germany (1976), France (1976), Denmark (1977) and The Netherlands (1975).

443. Downes, David (1988). *Contrasts in Tolerance: Post-war Penal Policy in the Netherlands and England and Wales*. New York: Clarendon Press, Oxford University Press. Bibliography, appendices, xii + 226pp.

Utilizes official and scholarly literature to compare changes in post-war penal and judicial trends in The Netherlands and England and Wales. Analyzes differential structural paradigms and judicial policies, decarceration theories, crime and drug control trends, and the effects of sentencing policies.

444. Dunkel, Frieder (1985). "Victim Compensation and Offender Restitution in the Federal Republic of Germany A Western-Euro-

pean Comparative Perspective," *International Journal of Comparative and Applied Criminal Justice*, 9(1): 29-39. Bibliography.

Outlines the growing social and legal trend toward victim compensation in the Federal Republic of Germany and compares its legislative application with various other countries in Europe. The latter include Britain, Denmark, Austria, Sweden, The Netherlands, Norway, Germany and France. Outlines The Victim Compensation Act of 1976 in the Federal Republic of Germany and discusses problems regarding victim compensation and offender restitution.

445. Dusan, Cotic (1988). *Drugs and Punishment*. Rome: United Nations Social Defence Research Institute. No.30. Charts, 146pp.

Surveys contemporary legislative and penal regulations for drug violations in Europe, Asia, Africa, and Latin America. Discussion focuses on methodological and drug related issues, national classification, and the implementation of policy changes. Outlines international penal regulations and crime rate statistics for drug violations.

446. Enker, Arnold N. (1974). "A Comparative Review of Compensation for Victims of Crime." Pp.121-138 in Israel Drapkin and Emilio Viano (eds.), *Victimology: A New Focus*, vol.2. Lexington, Massachusetts: Lexington Books and D.C. Heath. Annotations.

Reviews legal analogies and indemnity arguments and comparatively discusses legal and policy issues regarding systematic victim compensation schemes. Outlines victim compensations plans adopted in New Zealand, England, Israel, New South Wales, and the U.S. Discusses legal procedures and limitations.

447. Fenwick, Charles R. (1982). "Crime and Justice in Japan: Implications for the United States of America," *International Journal of Comparative and Applied Criminal Justice*, 6(1): 61-71. Bibliography.

Investigates the structural, cultural, and judicial forces that contribute to Japan's low crime rates. Focuses on social homogeneity, structural and social control processes, and cooperative judicial intervention. Outlines findings and suggests implications for the U.S.

448. Findlay, Mark, and Ugljesa Zvekic (eds.) (1988). *Informal Mechanisms of Crime Control: a Cross Cultural Perspective*. Rome: United Nations Social Defense Research Institute. No.31. Bibliography, 343pp.

A cross-cultural study of crime control in ten countries. Part 1 discusses the conceptual concerns and development of the project. Part 2 comprises nine articles, each describing various informal mechanisms of crime control in Saudi Arabia, West Africa, Italy, Morocco, Venezula, China, Japan, West Germany, Yugoslavia, and Egypt. Part 3 assesses the formalization of informal control mechanisms derived from data in Part 2.

449. Fooner, Michael (1989). *Interpol: Issues in World Crime and International Criminal Justice*. New York and London: Plenum Press. Notes, bibliography, appendices, xix + 244pp.

Offers a brief history of Interpol (International Criminal Police Organization) from 1923 to the present. Describes in detail its identity, governance, organization, the National Central Bureau, and the instruments and management of multinational police cooperation.

450. Fowles, A.J. (1989). *Prisoners' Rights in England and the United States.* Aldershot, Hants: Gower. Notes, bibliography, xv + 172pp.

Examines the philosophical context of prisoners' rights in the within the framework of human rights; protections and rights of English prisoners in domestic law and under European Convention; and prisoners' rights in the U.S. Final chapter offers explicit cross-cultural comparisons.

451. Frankowski, Stanislaw, and Eleonora Zielinska (1980). "Non-Custodial Penal Measures in European Socialist Countries," *International Review of Criminal Policy*, 36: 38-46. Annotations.

Reviews the possibilities of penal code alternatives to incarceration in several European socialist countries, including Poland, the U.S.S.R, Hungary, Czechoslovakia, and Bulgaria. Discusses the change from conventional to unsupervised socialist penal measures and profiles their incidence in Poland during the periods 1970-1972 and 1973 1975.

452. Gandy, John M. (1977). "Juvenile Justice in England and Scotland." Pp.17-21 in Paul C. Friday and V. Lorne Stewart (eds.), *Youth Crime and Juvenile Justice: International Perspectives.* New York: Praeger.

Compares basic social and cultural differences between England and Scotland's juvenile justice administration. Outlines changes in juvenile laws and judicial process. Briefly discusses the relationship between the juvenile justice system and the criminal justice process in both countries.

453. Gillespie, Robert W. (1981). "Sanctioning Traditional Crimes with Fines: A Comparative Analysis," *International Journal of Comparative and Applied Criminal Justice*, 5(2): 197-204. Bibliography.

Explores the variety of responses to alternative crime sanctions in England, Germany, Sweden, and the U.S. Focus is the use of fines as an alternative to incarceration. Discusses objective specification, critical review, crime and sanction comparability, social control features, and the economic advantages of fines. Findings and implications provided.

454. Grabosky, Peter N. (1984). "The Variability of Punishment." Pp.163-189 in vol.1 of Donald Black (ed.), *Toward a General Theory of Social Control.* 2 vols. Orlando, Florida: Academic Press. Bibliography.

Outlines and extends selected existing theories of punishment. Discusses forms of punishment. Analyzes variations in punishment intensity in a variety of societies according to social differentiation, centralization of authority, heterogeneity, situational stress, and economic constraints.

455. Graefrath, Bernhard (1989). "International Crimes A Specific Regime of International Responsibility of States and its Legal

Consequences." Pp.161-169 in Joseph H.H. Weiler, Antonio Cassese and Marina Spinedi (eds.), *International Crimes of State: A Critical Analysis of the ILC's Draft Article on State Responsibility.* Berlin: Walter de Gruyter. Annotations.

Critically explores the basic reasons for the legal distinction between state responsibility, interpreted as *erga omnes* obligations in international state crimes, and other violations of international law. Examines legal consequences of international state responsibility and the condition and extent of such consequences for those states not directly affected by international violations.

456. Griffiths, Curt Taylor, and L. Thomas Winfree (1982). "Attitudes Toward the Police: A Comparison of Canadian and American Adolescents," *International Journal of Comparative and Applied Criminal Justice*, 6(2): 127-141. Notes, bibliography.

Investigates and compares adolescent attitudes toward the police in Canada and the U.S. Outlines variation in responses of adolescent group samples. Findings in both countries suggest adolescent attitudes toward the police are strongly influenced by the type of communication experienced between adolescents and police. Details methodological design.

457. Hackler, Jim, Joan Brockman, and Eva Luczynska (1977). "The Comparison of Role Interrelationships in Two Juvenile Courts: Vienna and Boston," *International Journal of Criminology and Penology*, 5(4): 367-397. Bibliography.

Uses survey data to investigate and compare formal and semiformal interrelationships of juvenile court systems in Vienna, Austria, and Boston, Massachusetts. Outlines 'core' roles (judges), 'auxiliary' roles (defense attorneys), and 'supporting roles' (police) and their relationship to the juvenile court system. Discusses methodological design. Findings review cultural variation in juvenile court roles.

458. Hagan, John, and Jeffrey Leon (1978). "Philosophy and Sociology of Crime Control: Canadian-American Comparisons." Pp.181-208 in Harry M. Johnson (ed.), *Social System and Legal Process.* San Francisco, California: Jossey-Bass. Notes, bibliography.

Uses Canadian and U.S. literature from 1942 to 1976 to examine alternative crime control responses. Outlines due process and crime control as two crime response models. Compares the relationships among national values, historical practices, economic restraints, crime control, and due process. Reviews crime control philosophies, crime patterns, some historical cases, and findings. Provides U.S. and Canadian arrest ratios for burglary, homicide, forgery and counterfeiting, fraud and embezzlement, and theft and larceny from 1960 to 1970.

459. Hasson, Uzy, and Leslie Sebba (1974). "Compensation to Victims of Crime: A Comparative Survey." Pp.103-120 in vol.2 of Israel Drapkin and Emilio Viano (eds.), *Victimology: A New Focus.* 2 vols. Lexington, Massachusetts: Lexington Books and D.C. Heath. Annotations, appendix.

Reviews traditional compensation methods used by criminal courts and compares the evolution of state indemnity designs in England, Germany, Belgium, France, New Zealand, Australia, Northern Ireland, Israel, and the

U.S. Measures compensation distribution rates by offense type. Discusses weaknesses of existing compen sation models.

460. Hayakawa, Takeo, and John R. Schmidhauser (1987). "A Comparative Analysis of the Internal Procedures and Customs of the Supreme Courts of Japan and the United States." Pp.200-221 in John R. Schmidhauser (ed.), *Comparative Judicial Systems: Challenging Frontiers in Conceptual and Empirical Analysis*. London: Butterworths. Notes, bibliography.

Examines the internal procedures and customs of post-World War II Japanese and U.S. Supreme Courts. Sketches Japanese and U.S. judicial evolution. Compares legal, judicial, institutional, and organizational aspects of internal court procedures.

461. Iacovetta, R.G. (1981). "Research Problems and Issues in Comparative Corrections," *International Journal of Comparative and Applied Criminal Justice*, 5(2): 205-211. Bibliography.

Addresses the cultural and methodological difficulties encountered in the cross-cultural comparison of correctional systems. Illustrates the various obstructions to accurate comparative analysis through an assessment of penal systems in the U.S., Mexico, West Germany, England, Sweden, and Japan.

462. Johnson, Knowlton (1983). "Law Enforcement Selection Practices: The United States and Canada." Pp.103-119 in Israel L. Barak-Glantz and Elmer H. Johnson (eds.), *Comparative Criminology*. Beverly Hills, California: Sage. Notes, bibliography.

Provides a comparative introduction to philosophy and execution of law enforcement selection practices of police recruitment in the U.S. and Canada. Discusses methodological features, changes in personnel requirements, and similarities/dissimilarities in cultural practices.

463. Kravitz, Marjorie (ed.) (1978). *International Summaries: A Collection of Selected Translations in Law Enforcement and Criminal Justice*, vol. 1. Washington, D.C.: National Criminal Justice Reference Service. No. J26.17: 1.

This first volume in a continuing series of international criminological summaries. Includes 25 translated articles on political and terrorist crimes in West Germany and Spain; crime prevention procedures in West Germany and France; trends in corrections in Switzerland, Italy and other European nations; organizational and historical aspects of police functions in Japan, France, and West Germany; concepts about how to reform the criminal justice system in Venezuela; and functional aspects of crime reporting systems.

464. Kurian, George Thomas (1989). *World Encyclopedia of Police Forces and Penal Systems*. New York: Facts on File. Bibliography, appendices, viii + 582pp.

Describes various aspects of police forces and correctional systems in 183 countries. Each country entry contains demographic data ('Basic Fact Sheet'); information about the history, structure, organization, recruitment, education, and training of police; description of the penal system; and selected crime statistics.

465. Lee, Orlan, and T.A. Robertson (1973). *"Moral Order" and the Criminal Law: Reform Efforts in the United States and West Germany.* Netherlands: Martinus Nijhoff, The Hague. xxiv + 266pp.

Compares the development of criminal law reform in Germany and the U.S. Discusses constitutional and theoretical issues and how political, social, ethical, philosopical, and religious concepts have affected legal attitudes and legal development. Systematically reviews German and U.S. historical, political, judicial, and philosophical concepts of law and punishment.

466. Lenke, Leif (1980). "Criminal Policy and Repression in Capitalist Societies: the Scandinavian Case," *Scandinavian Studies in Criminology*, 7:5 30. Notes, bibliography.

Employs a conflict model to examine crime control strategies and police conduct. Tests the relationships among repressive penal policies in capitalist societies, levels of manifest political conflict, and class power differences in Denmark, Norway, Sweden, and Finland. Longitudinal analysis is used as basis of cross-cultural comparisons.

467. Leon, Jeffrey S. (1978). "Rights, Fairness and Effectiveness in Canada and the United States: Counsel and Client in the Criminal Process," *Criminal Law Quarterly*, 20(1): 29-67. Annotations.

Compares interpretational and procedural differences in the legal approaches toward due process in Canada and the U.S. Uses legal case studies to characterize Canadian and U.S. legal models and discusses legal representation and judicial practices of Canadian and U.S. attorneys and courts. Outlines the effects of incompetent legal representation and recommends changes to judicial guidelines.

468. Lōpez-Rey, Manuel (1985). *A Guide to United Nations Criminal Policy.* Brookfield, Vermont: Gower. Annex, xi + 142pp.

Describes the historical development of United Nations criminal policy and its involvement in identifying the crime rates of member countries. Addresses various problems within U.N. doctrine, including its constricted focus on specific types of crime and escalating global crime rates.

469. Los, Maria (1985). "The Myth of Popular Justice Under Communism: A Comparative View of the USSR and Poland," *Justice Quarterly*, 2(4): 447-471. Bibliography.

Describes, compares, and evaluates two popular justice institutions (workers' courts and residential tribunals) in U.S.S.R. and Poland. Assesses western and communist concepts of popular justice, theoretical and political aspects, judicial organization, and formal and informal procedural mechanisms.

470. Lutzker, Marilyn, and Eleanor Ferrall (1986). *Criminal Justice Research in Libraries: Strategies and Resources.* Westport, Connecticut: Greenwood Press. Appendices, xvi + 167pp.

Offers well-organized and practical guidance for the study of criminal justice and related disciplines. Provides research development, various discovery techniques, biographical information, and specialized research directives. Pp.125-133 ('Resources for the Study of Criminal Justice in Other Countries') contain information on overviews, bibliographies, periodical indices and abstracts, translations of foreign-language sources, news sources and public opinion polls, U.S. and foreign government documents, and statistical sources.

471. Lynch, James P. (1988). "A Comparison of Prison Use in England, Canada, West Germany, and the United States: A Limited Test of the Punitive Hypothesis," *Journal of Criminal Law and Criminology*, 79(1): 180 217. Annotations, appendices.

A cross-cultural examination of incarceration rates and punitiveness. Crimes examined include homicide, rape, robbery, aggravated assault, burglary, larceny, and motor vehicle theft. Countries compared are U.S., England, Canada, and West Germany. Describes methodological features and findings and discusses previous research designs. Addresses difficulties with comparative analysis.

472. Mannheim, Hermann (1958). "Comparative Sentencing Practice," *Law and Contemporary Problems*, 23(3): 557-582. Annotations.

Compares judicial sentencing practices in England and Wales, Scotland, Austria, Denmark, France, West Germany, Italy, the Netherlands, and Sweden during specific periods from 1909 to 1954. Examines a variety of crimes, including sexual/nonsexual crimes against the person, violent/nonviolent property crimes, and miscellaneous offenses. Surveys sentencing range, trends, and legal codes. Outlines social, economic, and structural factors that influence sentencing customs.

473. Marnell, Gunnar (1972). "Comparative Correctional Systems: United States and Sweden," *Criminal Law Bulletin*, 8(9): 748-760. Annotations.

Provides an informal comparison of U.S. and Swedish penal systems. Outlines the differences in historical features, correctional policies, physical, psychological and educational needs of prisoners, and social welfare institutions. Critically discusses the existence of undesirable prison conditions in the U.S.

474. Mueller, Gerhard O.W. (1983). "The United Nations and Criminology." Pp.63-81 in Elmer H. Johnson (ed.), *International Handbook of Contemporary Developments in Criminology: General Issues and the Americas*. Westport, Connecticut: Greenwood Press. Notes, bibliography.

Describes the organizational, judicial, and administrative structures and functions of the United Nations. Discusses the international functions of the Crime Prevention and Criminal Justice Branch of the United Nations, including international meetings and data gathering, distribution of data and their analysis. Outlines international crime rates for person, property, and drug related crimes in underdeveloped countries from 1970 to 1975. Contrasts these crime rates with those in developing countries.

475. Mueller, Gerhard O.W., Michael Gage, and Lenore R. Kupperstein (1969). *The Legal Norms of Delinquency: A Comparative Study*. New York: Criminal Law Education and Research Center. Annotations, 76pp.

An interdisciplinary study of juvenile offenses, legal and judicial procedure, adjudication processes, and corrections in Poland, Yugoslavia, Israel, and Puerto Rico. Compares findings with the state of Colorado. Describes methodology, terminology of criminal law, and official statistics.

476. Normandeau, André, and Burkhard Hasenpush (1981). "Crime and Delinquency Prevention in Some European Countries," *International Journal of Comparative and Applied Criminal Justice*, 5(1): 41-49. Bibliography.

Describes and compares crime prevention programs in Belgium, France, Germany, and Switzerland. Focuses on the systematic and operative features of prevention programs and methods of intervention, such as family case work, social organization, crisis intervention, and prevention assistance.

477. Parker, L. Craig Jr. (1984). *The Japanese Police System Today: An American Perspective.* Tokyo: Kodansha International. Notes, bibliography, 220pp.

An interdisciplinary book that examines the relationships among police, community membership, and low crime rates in Japan. Identifies, within a comparative framework, those features of Japanese society which contribute to its alleged low crime rates and model system of criminal justice. Provides some official data on international crime rates.

478. Parker, L. Craig Jr. (1986). *Parole and the Community Based Treatment of Offenders in Japan and the United States.* New Haven, Connecticut: University of New Haven Press. Bibliography, 156pp.

Compares criminal offender rehabilitation programs in Japan and the U.S. Discusses punishment and rehabilitative procedures and policy debates in both countries. Outlines differences in crime rates, incarceration, and recidivism. Provides penal code offenses and investigation rates in Japan between 1948 and 1981.

479. Peigne, Jean-Pierre (1982). "The Penalty of Law: An International Comparison of Practices Affecting the Prosecution and Sentencing of Juveniles," *International Summaries: A Series of Selected Translations in Law Enforcement and Criminal Justice.* NCJ-78589.

Reviews extant practices that influence juvenile prosecution and sentencing in various countries, including Brazil, Sri Lanka, Austria, Australia, Bangladesh, Japan, the German Federal Republic, Switzerland, and England and Wales. Discusses organizational problems of legal systems (e.g., juvenile proceedings) and variations in court functions (e.g. the contributory involvement of institutional agencies and rehabilitation programs).

480. Pfeffer, Richard M. (1970). "Crime and Punishment: China and the United States." Pp.261-281 in Jerome Alan Cohen (ed.), *Contemporary Chinese Law: Research Problems and Perspectives.* Cambridge, Massachusetts: Harvard University Press. Annotations.

Discusses different Chinese and American perspectives on law and judicial process. Outlines methodological and conceptual difficulties in comparative analysis of criminal law. Identifies various myths about criminal justice in the U.S. and examines China's commiytment to the ideal of substantive justice. Recommends aggregate judicial analysis.

481. Rahav, Giora (1983). "The Deterrent Effect of the Death Penalty: A Cross-National Study." Pp.193-203 in Giora S. Shoham (ed.), *The Many Faces of Crime and Deviance*. White Plains, New York: Sheridan House. Annotations.

Uses Interpol data and previous research to conduct a cross cultural analysis of the effect of the death penalty on murder and homicide. Outlines various methodological approaches to deterrence, including longitudinal studies, cross-sectional studies, and comparative studies. Compares homicide and murder rates for countries with and without capital punishment between 1965 and 1970. Findings suggest no direct relationship between the death penalty and murder and homicide rates.

482. Ross, Ruth A., and George C.S. Benson (1979). "Criminal Justice from East to West," *Crime and Delinquency*, 25(1): 76-86. Annotations.

Reviews criminal justice procedures in England, Japan, and the U.S. and compares official crime rates for homicide, robbery, and rape in New York, London, and Toyko. Discusses aspects of English and Japanese law enforcement and education, such as legal centralization and public awareness and participation, which may encourage a reduction in violent crime rates.

483. Sandhu, Harjit S. (1972). "Perceptions of Prison Guards: A Cross-National Study of India and Canada," *International Review of Modern Sociology*, 2:26-32. Bibliography.

Examines attitudes of prison guards towards their work, and their perceptions of the possibility of inmate reformation. Data derived from random sample questionnaire distributed to guards. Findings suggest that guards view reformation more favorably if they are older, more trained, more educated, and experienced.

484. Schmidhauser, John R. (1987). "Alternative Conceptual Frameworks in Comparative Cross-National Legal and Judicial Research." Pp.34-58 in John R. Schmidhauser (ed.), *Comparative Judicial Systems: Challenging Frontiers in Conceptual and Empirical Analysis*. London: Butterworths. Notes, bibliography.

Critically explores alternative conceptual frameworks for the comparative examination of judicial systems. Criticizes several comparative law theses, especially that of the German sociologist Max Weber.

485. Schumann, Karl F. (1983). "Comparative Research on Legal Sanctions: Problems and Proposals," *International Journal of the Sociology of Law*, 11(3): 267-276. Bibliography.

Questions the utility of incarceration rates in historical and/or comparative analysis. Critically outlines historical and cross-cultural research on legal sanctions. Exemplifies some methodological difficulties of using incarceration rates in comparative research and the need for comprehensive measures of penal sanctions. Provides brief recommendations for future analysis.

486. Schur, Edwin M. (1962). *Narcotic Addiction in Britain and America: The Impact of Public Policy*. Bloomington, Indiana: Indiana University Press. Bibliography, appendices, 281pp.

Investigates British and U.S. drug policies. Identifies and discusses the functional aspects of Britain's drug policy and questions its suitability for the U.S. Reviews five British addiction cases. Appendices outline methodological details.

487. Shane, Paul G. (1980). *People and Police: A Comparision of Five Countries*. St. Louis, Missouri: C.V. Mosby. Bibliography, appendices, 219pp.

Compares the organization and development and functions of the police in Britain, India, Israel, The Netherlands, and the U.S. Outlines historical and sytematic variations in police forces. Methodological design, findings and indications provided. Appendices review official police data.

488. Sieverdes, Christopher, and Clemens Bartollas (1977). "Modes of Adaptation and Game Behavior at Two Juvenile Institutions." Pp.22-38 in Paul C. Friday and V. Lorne Stewart (eds.), *Youth Crime and Juvenile Justice: International Perspectives*. New York: Praeger. Bibliography.

Compares methods of adaptation and game play behavior used by juvenile inmates in two youth coeducational schools in a south-eastern state in the U.S. Discusses adjustment classification, behavioral characterization of incarcerated youths, and inmate and staff interaction. Methodological design describes sample selection, survey technique, and the application of Robert Merton's typology.

489. Smith, Harold (ed.) (1989). *Transnational Crime: Investigative Responses*. Chicago, Illinois: Office of International Criminal Justice. Notes, annotations, bibliographies, x + 136pp.

Sixteen short chapters written by authors from seven countries. Addresses a wide variety of problems in international law enforcement, including crimes with an international character, international agencies such as Interpol, the police, and technological innovation and research.

490. Solheim, Joan Senzek (1982). "A Cross-Cultural Examination of Use of Corporal Punishment on Children: A Focus on Sweden and the United States," *Child Abuse and Neglect*, 6: 147-154. Bibliography.

Examines the physical punishment of children in Sweden and the U.S. Focus is cultural variation in corporal punishment exercised by parents and school personnel. Outlines demographic features, child abuse statistics, child mortality rates, and social and legal ideologies in both countries. Advocates the adoption of Swedish standards in the U.S.

491. Stevens, James W., and David W. MacKenna (1985). "A Comparative Analysis of Criminal Investigator Training in the United

States and West Germany," *International Journal of Comparative and Applied Criminal Justice*, 9(2): 35-43. Bibliography.

Examines criminal investigator training programs in the U.S. and West Germany. Compares historical and structural features of police systems, training, qualifications, and performance assessment.

492. Stevens, James W., and Pattye Sue Aldrich (1985). "The Integration of Women into West German and United States Police Service," *International Journal of Comparative and Applied Criminal Justice*, 9(1): 57-66. Bibliography.

Compares contemporary gender roles and the traditional ideology of female participation in law enforcement employment in West Germany and the U.S. Compares job description and social role status of female and male police officers in both countries. Includes methodological outline of the study.

493. Terrill, Richard J. (1984). *World Criminal Justice Systems: A Survey*. Cincinnati, Ohio: Anderson. Bibliography, xiv + 417pp.

Promotes a descriptive, macro-comparative approach to the study of criminal justice in England, France, Sweden, Japan, and the U.S.S.R. Discusses the utility of comparative analysis, methodological models and limitations, and the operative legal and criminal justice systems in these five countries. Some comparisons with the U.S. are provided.

494. Trebach, Arnold S. (1982). *The Heroin Solution*. New Haven, Connecticut: Yale University Press. Annotations, xvi + 331pp.

A wide-ranging analysis of heroin epidemics and government responses from early 1900s to the present. Many sections of the book entail comparative generalizations about the respective medical and criminal law models of Britain and the U.S.

495. Waller, Louis (1974). "Compensating the Victims of Crime in Australia and New Zealand." Pp.175-192 in Israel Drapkin and Emilio Viano (eds.), *Victimology: A New Focus*, vol.2. Lexington, Massachusetts: Lexington Books and D.C. Heath. Annotations.

Reviews Australian and New Zealand indemnity statutes and compares their respective legal enactment of official state involvement in criminal injuries. Discusses the rationale for compensation statutes. Outlines compensation schemes and practices for both countries and offers impressions about the future of compensation laws.

496. Wasikhongo, Joab M.N. (1976). "The Role and Character of Police in African and Western Countries: A Comparative Approach to Police Isolation," *International Journal of Criminology and Penology*, 4(4): 383-396. Bibliography.

Utilizes field study data to compare the origin and nature of police-public isolation in Uganda, Nigeria, Kenya, India, the U.S., Britain, and Australia. Police-public isolation is held to derive from historical factors, from differences between police practices and public expectations, from centralization, and from the structural nature of police organizations.

497. Weiler, Joseph H.H., Antonio Cassese and Marina Spinedi (eds.) (1989). *International Crimes of State: A Critical Analysis of the ILC's Draft Article 19 on State Responsibility.* Berlin: Walter de Gruyter. 368pp.

A comprehensive set of 41 conference papers focusing on the conceptual interpretation of that part of Article 19 found in the International Law Commission which addresses international crimes of state. Papers discuss legislative history, state conflict and responsibility regarding Article 19, international concepts of state crimes, and interpretation of the International Law Commission (ILC). Includes international crimes of state bibliography for 1946-1984 and draft articles.

498. Wickman, Peter (1983). "Role Conflicts and Stress of Prison Guards: Organizational and Cross National Perspectives." Pp.135-155 in Israel L. Barak-Glantz and Elmer H. Johnson (eds.), *Comparative Criminology.* Beverly Hills, California: Sage. Bibliography.

Uses an organizational approach and secondary cross-cultural data to examine the links between stress suffered by prison guards and the structural, institutional, and environmental aspects of their role conflict in the U.S., Finland, Sweden, and Denmark. Details organizational aspects of prisons and describes methodology and findings.

499. Wicks, Robert J., and H.H.A. Cooper (eds.) (1979). *International Corrections.* Lexington, Massachusetts: Lexington Books and D.C. Heath. Annotations, x + 189pp.

This collection of 12 single culture essays discusses correctional systems in England and Wales, Canada, the Federal Republic of Germany, France, Latin America, Mexico, Finland, Israel, Japan, and Nigeria. Addreses historical and contemporary perspectives, juvenile and adult penal law, and changes in correctional practices. Provides some conviction and parole rates.

500. Zvekic, Ugljesa and Aurelio Mattei (1987). *Research and International Co-operation in Criminal Justice: Survey on Needs and Priorities of Developing Countries.* Pub.29. Rome: United Nations Social Defence Research Institute. Charts, 264pp.

Relies on the findings of three UNSDRI surveys conducted in 1976, 1982, and 1986 to examine crime in developing countries. Examines the priorities of developing countries, issues regarding crime categories and criminal justice systems, and international cooperation. Offers global and regional levels of analysis. Outlines countries that participated in all three surveys and offers international comparisons. Methodological and conceptual difficulties addressed.

APPENDICES

Appendix A: Lists of Countries in Cross-National Data Sets

1. *The Comparative Crime Data File*. Pp.171-328 in Dane Archer and Rosemary Gartner, *Violence and Crime in Cross-National Perspective* (1984), New Haven, Connecticut: Yale University Press. [See also # 080].

   (a) Countries: Aden, Argentina, Australia, Austria, Bahrain, Belgium, Bermuda, Bolivia, Botswana, Brunei, Bulgaria, Burma, Cameroon, Canada, Central African Republic, Chad, Chile, China (Republic of), Colombia, Congo (Brazzaville), Cuba, Cyprus, Dahomey, Denmark, Dominican Republic, Egypt, El Salvador, England (and Wales), Ethiopia, Fiji, Finland, France, Germany, Ghana, Greece, Guam, Guyana, Hong Kong, Hungary, Iceland, India, Indonesia, Iran, Iraq, Ireland (Eire), Israel, Italy, Ivory Coast, Jamaica, Japan, Jordan, Kenya, Khmer Republic (Cambodia), Korea, Kuwait, Laos, Lebanon, Libya, Luxembourg, Malagasy Republic, Malawi (Nyasaland), Mauritania, Mauritius, Mexico, Monaco, Morocco, Nepal, Netherlands, Netherlands Antilles, New Zealand, Nigeria, Northern Ireland, Norway, Pakistan, Panama, Peru, Philippines, Poland, Portugal, Puerto Rico, Qatar, Rhodesia, Rumania, Scotland, Senegal, Sierra Leone, Singapore, Solomon Islands, South Africa, Spain, Sri Lanka (Ceylon), Sudan, Surinam, Swaziland, Sweden, Switzerland, Syria, Tangiers, Tanzania, Thailand, Trinidad and Tobago, Tunisia, Turkey, Uganda, United States, Venezuela, Vietnam (South), West Indies (British), Yugoslavia, and Zambia.

   (b) International Cities: Accra, Amsterdam, Athens, Beirut, Belfast, Bombay, Brussels, Calcutta, Caracas, Colombo City, Daho City, Dublin, Freetown, Georgetown, Glasgow, Helsinki, Istanbul, Jerusalem, Johannesburg, Khartoum, Kuwait City, Lagos City, Madrid, Manila, Mexico City, Montevideo, Munich, Nairobi City, New York City, Oslo, Panama City, Paris, Port of Spain, Quezon City, Salisbury, Seoul, Stockholm, Sydney, Tananarive, Tokyo, Vienna, Warsaw, Wellington, and Zurich.

2. *Correlates of Crime*. In Richard R. Bennett, *Correlates of Crime: A Study of Nations, 1960-1984* (1989), Ann Arbor, Michigan: Interuniversity Consortium for Political and Social Research, ICPSR No. 9258. [See also # 082].

   Countries: Australia, Austria, Brunei, Burma, Canada, Chile, Cyprus, Denmark, Egypt, England (and Wales), Fiji, Finland, France, Germany (West), Greece, Hong Kong, India, Indonesia, Israel, Italy, Ivory Coast, Jamaica, Japan, Kenya, Korea, Kuwait, Lebanon, Libya, Luxembourg, Malawi, Malaysia, Morocco, Monaco, Netherlands, New Zealand, Nigeria, Norway, Peru, Philippines, Portugal, Scotland, Singapore, Spain, Sri Lanka, Sweden, Syria, Taiwan, Tanzania, Turkey, United States, West Indies, and Zambia.

3. In Ted Robert Gurr (1977). "Crime Trends in Modern Democracies Since 1945," *Annales Internationales de Criminologie*, 16(1-2): 41-85. [See also # 096].

   Countries: Austria, Canada, Denmark, England and Wales, Finland, France, Ireland, Israel, Italy, Japan, Netherlands, Norway, Sweden, Switzerland, U.S., and West Germany.

4. World Health Organization (1921-). "Homicide Statistics." In *World Health Statistic Annual Annuaire de statistiques sanitaires mondiales*. Geneva: World Health Organization. [See also # 116]

   Countries: Australia, Austria, Belgium, Brazil, Bulgaria, Canada, Chile, China, Costa Rica, Cuba, Czechoslovakia, Denmark, Ecuador, England and Wales, Finland, France, German Democratic Republic, Hungary, Iceland, Ireland, Italy, Japan, Korea (Republic of), Luxembourg, Malta, Mexico, Netherlands, Northern Ireland, Norway, Panama, Poland, Portugal, Puerto Rico, Scotland, Spain, Sweden, Switzerland, Turkey, U.S., and the U.S.S.R.

   Note: Countries included vary from one year to another.

5. Interpol (1950/1951-). *International Crime Statistics*. Paris: International Criminal Police Organization. [See also # 098].

   Countries: Angola, Argentina, Australia, Austria, Bahamas, Bahrain, Barbados, Belgium, Botswana, Brunei, Burkina Faso, Burma, Burundi, Canada, Cayman Islands, Chile, China, Congo, Costa Rica, Cote d'Ivoire, Cyprus, Denmark, Dominica, Dominican Republic, Ecuador, Ethiopia, Fiji, Finland, Gabon, Germany (Federal Republic of), Greece, Grenada, Guyana, Honduras, Hong Kong, Hungary, India, Indonesia, Ireland, Israel, Italy, Jamaica, Japan, Jordan, Kenya, Korea (Republic of), Kuwait, Lebanon, Lesotho, Libya, Luxembourg, Malawi, Malaysia, Maldives, Mali, Malta, Mauritius, Mexico, Monaco, Morocco, Nepal, Netherlands, New Zealand, Norway, Pakistan, Panama, Papua New Guinea, Peru, Philippines, Portugal, Qatar, Rwanda, Saudi Arabia, Senegal, Seychelles, Singapore, Somalia, Spain, Sri Lanka, St.Lucia, Sudan, Sweden, Switzerland, Syria, Tanzania, Thailand, Trinidad and Tobago, Tunisia, United Arab Emirates, United Kingdom (England and Wales, and Northern Ireland), United States, Venezuela, Yugoslavia, Zambia, and Zimbabwe.

   Note: Countries included vary from one year to another.

Appendix B: Lists of United Nations Interregional Crime and Justice Research Institute Publications and Staff Papers

(a) List of Publications

Publ. No.1 F. Ferracuti and R. Bergalli (1969). *Tendencias y necesidades de la investigación criminológica en America Latina.*

Publ. No.2 F. Ferracuti and M.C. Giannini (1970). *Manpower and training in the field of social defence.*

Publ. No.3 (1971). *Social defence in Uganda: a survey of research.*

Publ. No.4 A. Bouhdiba (1971). *Public et justice: une étude pilote en Tunisie.*

Publ. No.5 (1973). *Migration.* Report of the Research Conference on Migration, Ethnic Minority Status and Social Adaptation, Rome, 13-16 June, 1972

Publ. No.6 (1973). *A programme for drug use research.* Report of the proceedings of a workshop at Frascati, Italy, 11-15 December, 1972.

Publ. No.7 B. Kasme (ed.) (1974). *A world directory of Criminological Institutes.*

Publ. No.8 (1974). *Recent contributions to Soviet criminology.*

Publ. No.9 (1974). *Economic crisis and crime. Interim report and materials.*

Publ. No.10 (1974). *Criminological research and decision making. Studies on the influence of criminological research on criminal policy in The Netherlands and Finland.*

Publ. No.11 (1976). *Evaluation research in criminal justice.* Material and proceedings of a research conference convened in the context of the Fifth United Nations Congress on the Prevention of Crime and the Treatment of Offenders.

Publ. No.12 (1976). *Juvenile justice. An international survey, country reports, related materials and suggestions for future research.*

Publ. No.13 (1976). *The protection of the artistic and archaeological heritage. A view from Italy and India.*

Publ. No.14 (1976). *Prison architecture. An international survey of representative closed institutions and analysis of current trends in prison design.*

Publ. No.15 (1976). *Economic crises and crime. Correlations between the state of the economy, deviance and the control of crime.*

Publ. No.16 J.J. Moore (1976). *Investigating drug abuse. A multinational programme of pilot studies into the non-medical use of drugs.*

Publ. No.17 (1978). *A world directory of criminological institutes.* 2nd edition.

Publ. No.18 S.K. Mukherjee and A. Gupta (1978). *Delay in the administration of criminal justice India.*

Publ. No.19 J.J. Moore and and L. Bozzetti (1979). *Research and drug policy.*

Publ. No.20 (1982). *A world directory of criminological institutes.* 3rd edition.

Publ. No.21 F. Bruno (1984). *Combatting drug abuse.*

Publ. No.22 (1984). *Juvenile social maladjustment and human rights in the context of urban development.*

Publ. No.23 I.F. Caramazza and U. Leone (1984). *The phenomenology of kidnappings in Sardinia.*

Publ. No.24 (1984). *The rôle of the judge in contemporary society.*

Publ. No.25 P. David (ed.) (1985). *Crime and criminal policy. Papers in honour of Manuel López-Rey.*

Publ. No.26 (1985). *First Joint International Conference on Research in Crime prevention.* Riyad, 23-25 January, 1984.

Publ. No.27 U. Zvekic (ed.) (1986). *Action-oriented research on youth crime: an international perspective.*

Publ. No.28 C. Masotti Santoro (ed.) (1986). *A world directory of criminological institutes.* 4th edition.

Publ. No.29 U. Zvekic and A. Mattei (1987). *Research and international cooperation in criminal justice: Survey on needs and priorities of developing countries.*

Publ. No.30 D. Cotic (1988). *Drugs and punishment.*

Publ. No.31 M. Findlay and U. Zvekic (1988). *Analyzing (in)formal mechanisms of crime control: A cross cultural perspective.*

Publ. No.32 (1988). *The death penalty: A bibliographical research.*

Publ. No.33 L. Aniyar de Castro (ed.) (n.d.). *La criminologia en América Latina.*

Publ. No.34 L. Aniyar de Castro (ed.) (n.d.). *Criminology in Latin America.*

(b) List of Staff Papers

S.P. No.1 F. Ferracuti (1971). "Co-ordination of interdisciplinary research in criminology."

S.P. No.2 R.W. Burnham (1972). "The evaluation and improvement of manpower training programmes in social defence."

S.P. No.3 G. Newman (1972). "Perceptions of deviance. Suggestions for cross-cultural research."

S.P. No.4 F. Ferracuti and G. Newman (1973). "Perception clinique et psychologique de la déviance."

S.P. No.5 J.J. Moore, C.R.B. Joyce and J. Woodcock (1973). "Psychoactive drug control. Issues and recommendations."

S.P. No.6 (1973). "Un programma di ricerca sulla droga. Rapporto del seminario di Frascati," 11-15 December, 1972.

(c) Miscellaneous uncategorized publications

(n.d.). G. Newman. "Sexual deviance. A sociological analysis."

(n.d.). F. Ferracuti and R. Lazzari. "Aspetti sociali dei comportamenti devianti sessuali."

(1981). "The effect of Islamic legislation on crime prevention in Saudi Arabia."

Appendix C: Addresses of United Nations Regional Institutes for Crime Prevention

1) United Nations Asia and Far East Institute for the Prevention of Crime and the Treatment of Offenders (UNAFEI) 1-26 Harumicho, Futhu, Tokyo, Japan

2) United Nations Latin American Institute for the Prevention of Crime and the Treatment of Delinquency (ILANUD) San Josê 10071, 1000 San Josê, Costa Rica

3) United Nations African Regional Institute for the Prevention of Crime (UNAFRI) c/o UNDP Field Office, P.O. Box 7184, Kampala, Uganda

4) Helsinki Institute for Crime Prevention and Control (HEUNI) P.O. Box 34, SF 00931 Helsinki, Finland

5) United Nations Interregional Crime and Justice Research Institute (UNICRI) Via Giulia 52, I-00186 Rome, Italy

Appendix D: Miscellaneous Research Aids

(1) Brief list of abstracts, indexes, and journals with relevance for comparative criminology

Abstracts: *Criminal Justice Abstracts*; *Criminology and Penology Abstracts*; *Police Science Abstracts*.

Indexes: *Criminal Justice Periodical Index*; *Current Law Index*; *Index to Legal Periodicals*; *Social Science Citation Index*.

Journals: *American Journal of Sociology*; *American Sociological Review*; *British Journal of Criminology*; *C.J. International*; *Contemporary Crises*; *Criminology*; *International Journal of Comparative and Applied Criminal Justice*; *International Journal of the Sociology of Law*; *Law & Society; Review Research in Law; Deviance and Social Control*; *Social Justice*.

(2) *Amnesty International. 1962-1987*. Leiden, The Netherlands: I.D.C. (1989-) Previously issued as two separate guides: Amnesty International publications; and Amnesty International country dossiers. Includes published and unpublished research material on political prisoners and abuses of civil rights thoughout the world. [See also # 139].

(3) The United Nations Criminal Justice Information Network

The United Nations Criminal Justice Information Network (UNCJIN) was established by the United Nations in 1989 to provide for the dissemination of criminal justice research, crime prevention programs, and crime control policies of member states. Services available include public information exchange; direct communication with all U.N. Regional Institutes and direct access to all other U.N. networks; searchable data bases of international crime statistics and other criminal justice data; legislative updates from around the world; calendar of events and meetings; and gateways to other commercial information services. Membership is open to all individuals and organizations. Contact: Graeme Newman, UNCJIN Coordinator, School of Criminal Justice, SUNY at Albany, 135 Western Avenue, Albany, N.Y. 12222.

Author Index

Note: In the index below numbers in boldface refer to page numbers in the appendices; all other numbers refer to entry numbers in the bibliography.

Subject Index

Note: In the index below numbers in boldface refer to page numbers in the appendices; all other numbers refer to entry numbers in the bibliography.

About the Compilers

PIERS BEIRNE, Professor of Sociology and Legal Studies at the University of Southern Maine, is the author of *Criminology* (1991), *Revolution in Law: Contributions to the Development of Soviet Legal Theory, 1917-1938* (1990), and *Marxism and Law* (1982), among other works.

JOAN HILL is a graduate of the Criminology Program at the University of Southern Maine.